DRAMA CLASSICS

The Drama Classics series aims to offer the world's greatest plays in affordable paperback editions for students, actors and theatregoers. The hallmarks of the series are accessible introductions, uncluttered texts and an overall theatrical perspective.

Given that readers may be encountering a particular play for the first time, the introduction seeks to fill in the theatrical/historical background and to outline the chief themes rather than concentrate on interpretational and textual analysis. Similarly the play-texts themselves are free of footnotes and other interpolations: instead there is an end-glossary of 'difficult' words and phrases.

The texts of the English-language plays in the series have been prepared taking full account of all existing scholarship. The foreign-language plays have been newly translated into a modern English that is both actable and accurate: many of the translators regularly have their work staged professionally.

Edited until his early death by Kenneth McLeish, the Drama Classics series continues with his aim of providing a first-class library of dramatic literature representing the best of world theatre.

Associate editors:
Professor Trevor R. Griffiths
Dr. Colin Counsell
School of Arts and Humanities
University of North London

DRAMA CLASSICS *the first hundred*

The Alchemist
All for Love
Andromache
Antigone
Arden of Faversham
Bacchae
Bartholomew Fair
The Beaux Stratagem
The Beggar's Opera
Birds
The Changeling
A Chaste Maid in
    Cheapside
The Cherry Orchard
Children of the Sun
El Cid
The Country Wife
Cyrano de Bergerac
The Dance of Death
The Devil is an
    Ass
Doctor Faustus
A Doll's House
Don Juan
The Duchess of
    Malfi
Edward II
Electra (Euripides)
Electra (Sophocles)
An Enemy of the
    People
Every Man in his
    Humour
Everyman
The Father
Faust
A Flea in her Ear
Frogs
Fuenteovejuna
The Game of Love
    and Chance

Ghosts
The Government
    Inspector
Hedda Gabler
The Hypochondriac
The Importance of
    Being Earnest
An Ideal Husband
An Italian Straw Hat
The Jew of Malta
The Knight of the
    Burning Pestle
The Lady from the Sea
The Learned Ladies
Life is a Dream
The Lower Depths
The Lucky Chance
Lulu
Lysistrata
The Magistrate
The Malcontent
The Man of Mode
The Marriage of Figaro
Mary Stuart
The Master Builder
Medea
The Misanthrope
The Miser
Miss Julie
A Month in the
    Country
A New Way to Pay Old
    Debts
Oedipus at Kolonos
Oedipus the King
The Oresteia
Peer Gynt
Phèdre
Philoctetes
The Playboy of the
    Western World

The Recruiting
    Officer
The Revenger's
    Tragedy
The Rivals
The Roaring Girl
The Robbers
La Ronde
Rosmersholm
The Rover
The School for
    Scandal
The Seagull
The Servant of Two
    Masters
She Stoops to Conquer
The Shoemaker's
    Holiday
The Spanish Tragedy
Spring's Awakening
Tartuffe
Thérèse Raquin
Three Sisters
'Tis Pity She's a Whore
Too Clever by Half
Ubu
Uncle Vanya
Vassa Zheleznova
Volpone
The Way of the World
The White Devil
The Wild Duck
Women Beware
    Women
Women of Troy
Woyzeck

*The publishers welcome
suggestions for further titles*

DRAMA CLASSICS

DOCTOR FAUSTUS

by
Christopher Marlowe

with an introduction by
Simon Trussler

London
NICK HERN BOOKS

www.nickhernbooks.co.uk

A Drama Classic

This edition of *Doctor Faustus* first published in Great Britain
as a paperback original in 1996 by Nick Hern Books Limited,
14 Larden Road, London W3 7ST

Reprinted 2000

Copyright in the introduction © 1996 Nick Hern Books Limited

The play text is reproduced from the 'Revels Plays' edition of
Doctor Faustus, published by Manchester University Press,
copyright © 1993 by David Bevington and Eric Rasmussen.
The complete scholarly edition is available from Manchester
University Press, Oxford Road, Manchester M13 9NR, UK

Typeset by Country Setting, Kingsdown, Kent CT14 8ES
Printed by Bath Press, Avon

A CIP catalogue record for this book is available from the
British Library

ISBN 1 85459 335 8

Introduction

Christopher Marlowe (1564-1593)

Christopher Marlowe was the second of nine children of a Canterbury shoemaker. Born in 1564, the same year as Shakespeare, he attended King's School, Canterbury, before entering Corpus Christi College, Cambridge, on a six-year scholarship intended to lead to Holy Orders. He duly achieved his BA Degree in 1584, but was awarded his MA in 1587 only following the Privy Council's insistence. During the intervening three years he is thought to have been acting as a government spy against the French, in the Catholic seminary at Rheims.

Marlowe was probably in London later in 1587 for the first staging of the two parts of his heroic drama *Tamburlaine the Great*, but it is uncertain whether *Doctor Faustus* followed in 1588 or was first performed as late as 1593. The dates of his other plays – *The Jew of Malta*, *Edward II* and *The Massacre of Paris* – are also conjectural, though their number suggests a young dramatist pursuing a busy stage career. Yet hints of a darker side to Marlowe's life persist. In 1589 he was briefly imprisoned in Newgate with his friend, the poet Thomas Watson, who had killed an innkeeper's son in a street brawl. Three years later he was fined and bound over to keep the peace for assaulting two constables in Shoreditch – yet was also apparently back in government service, as a messenger during the siege of Rouen.

A fellow writer, Robert Greene, attacked Marlowe around this time for 'diabolical atheism' (the book's publisher apparently censoring yet more scandalous allegations). Then, in 1593, the dramatist Thomas Kyd, arrested for possessing atheistical writings, alleged that these had belonged to Marlowe, also accusing his former friend of treason and sodomy. Summoned to appear before the Privy Council, Marlowe was examined on 20 May, released on bail, and ten days later stabbed to death by Ingram Frizer in a house or tavern in Deptford, south east of London. A dispute over the reckoning had allegedly been the cause, and Frizer was pardoned following a coroner's finding of 'homicide in self-defence'. On the day of Marlowe's burial, in an unmarked grave in Deptford parish church, a note was delivered to the authorities from the informer Richard Baines, 'concerning his damnable judgement of religion and scorn of God's word'.

What Happens in the Play

The learned Doctor Faustus, discovered in his study in the University of Wittenberg, is bored with orthodox scholarship, and plans to seek the rewards of magic. He conjures the Devil's servant Mephistopheles, who acts as an intermediary with Satan in the signing of a pact whereby Mephistopheles is to attend Faustus and do his bidding for twenty-four years, after which he will render up his immortal soul to Hell. Despite a Good Angel urging him to repentance, Faustus attends instead to the Bad Angel's persuasions – although, in the event, his interrogations of Mephistopheles teach him little that he did not know, and his adventures offer more spectacle than fulfilment. Having been entertained by a parade of the Seven Deadly Sins, Faustus is taken to Rome to play tricks on the Pope, and then visits the Emperor's court, where he humiliates a sceptical knight. Returning to Wittenberg, he conjures up the silent form of Helen of Troy and is so enraptured by her beauty that, despite the pleas of an Old Man to save his soul, he demands her simulated spirit, or succuba, as his mistress. As the end of his contracted term approaches, Faustus bids farewell to his fellow scholars, and ekes out a final, desperate hour, unable to implore the divine mercy of which he remains lingeringly aware. As the clock strikes midnight, he is carried away by devils to Hell.

Marlowe and the Emergence of Elizabethan Theatre

The professional London theatre was barely out of its infancy when Christopher Marlowe began to write for the stage. The first purpose-built playhouse in London, called simply the Theatre, had opened just a decade earlier, in 1576, and the Curtain soon followed. Both were situated in London's earliest 'theatre district' of Shoreditch, though later the Bankside in Southwark was often preferred. Both these outlying areas were beyond the jurisdiction of the City of

London, whose rulers believed that playgoing encouraged immoral behaviour, and helped to spread the plague. It was only after a long closure on account of plague, in 1594, that two outstanding companies emerged to begin their long-lasting rivalry – the Lord Chamberlain's Men (later the King's), with whom Shakespeare worked for all but the earliest years of his theatrical career, and the Lord Admiral's Men (later Prince Henry's), under the management of the impresario Philip Henslowe. Henslowe's so-called *Diaries* give us an account of performances and some intriguing insights into theatrical practices and finances from 1592 onwards, but unfortunately there are no such records for most of Marlowe's career, and the rapidly changing state of companies and allegiances at the time – combined with the periods of closure during the plague years of 1592–94 – further confuse the situation.

Though products of this period of upheaval, Marlowe's plays are firmly linked with the rising fortunes of Henslowe and his leading player (and later son-in-law), Edward Alleyn. Henslowe had built his first theatre, the Rose, on Bankside in 1589, and it was here, after the carrying out of extensive alterations and improvements three years later, that he installed a permanent acting company, the Admiral's Men, whom we know to have performed *Doctor Faustus* in 1594. An earlier company of Admiral's Men had probably performed both parts of *Tamburlaine* in 1588, and perhaps *Doctor Faustus* too, while a short-lived company of Strange's Men, who appear to have joined forces with the Admiral's on occasion, may have been the first to play *The Jew of Malta*. Both companies apparently contributed actors to a group of Pembroke's Men who toured the provinces, probably with *Edward II* in their repertoire, during the plague closure. By the time Henslowe's records become available, Alleyn was making all the great Marlovian heroes his own.

Marlowe's Faustus, as also the roles of Tamburlaine and Barabas, assume a style of playing which, though impossible to verify with any accuracy, was rooted rather in rhetorical skill than psychological understanding. It's worth noting that the word 'acting' was employed at this time to describe the *gestic* component of a player's skills – an aspect of that 'presentational' style, out-front to the audience, that the long and often quite formal speeches of *Doctor Faustus* seem to require. A new term, 'personation', came into use around the turn of the century, as if needed to distinguish the more intimate and reciprocal manner, and more detailed approach to character-drawing, developed by Richard Burbage for his great Shakespearean roles.

Both actors had, of course, to contend with the elements (as well as the audiences) in the open-air theatres: here, the 'groundlings' stood on three sides of a raised platform stage, and protection from the weather was only to be found in the higher-priced seats of the galleries, whose tiers formed the theatre's perimeter. After 1609, when adult companies began also to perform at indoor, 'private' playhouses, it is argued that plays were specifically targeted to appeal to the more socially-elite audience of those theatres: but when Marlowe was writing no such distinction had arisen. Rich and poor, learned and illiterate, attended the same playhouses and enjoyed the same repertoire of plays.

The unsettled state of the theatre during Marlowe's short creative lifetime was to some extent reflected in his dramaturgy – but the changing structures and thematic concerns of his plays do not necessarily imply a developmental progress from 'primitive' to 'sophisticated'. The techniques and conventions of the earlier Tudor drama – notably the moral and secular interludes – suggest a skilful use of available resources, and a complex theatricalisation of shared assumptions. Among Marlowe's plays, *Doctor Faustus* is most clearly indebted to that tradition.

In the sheer scope and technical accomplishment of his plays, Marlowe marked out new ground for the Elizabethan drama – as he did, too, in his use of the medium of blank verse, in which he recognised (though he did not create) what was to become the distinctive dramatic idiom of the age. Marlowe's 'mighty line', as Ben Jonson famously called it, resonated most clearly and with least complicated rhetorical vigour in *Tamburlaine*, and achieved what Eliot called 'a gain in intensity' and 'a new and important conversational tone' in *Doctor Faustus*: then, in *The Jew of Malta* and *Edward II*, Marlowe went on to explore its more dialectical strengths, as a medium for the fully flexible and reciprocal dialogue of those plays. But such a sense of Marlowe's 'development' as a dramatist depends upon a chronology which, as we shall see, remains controversial as well as largely conjectural.

The Date and Sources of *Doctor Faustus*

The performances at the Rose in 1594 are the first references we have to the playing of *Doctor Faustus*. The Admiral's Men perhaps purchased the prompt-book from a company of Pembroke's Men, which may have performed the play at court during the Christmas celebrations of 1592, and at the Theatre in Shoreditch during a brief abatement of the plague in 1593. It remains uncertain whether the play dates from 1593, and so represents the culmination of Marlowe's brief dramatic career, or, as I myself believe, was a product of the late 1580s, and thus written soon after *Tamburlaine*. But we do know that *Doctor Faustus* remained in the repertoire of the Admiral's Men at least until 1597, and that a revival in 1602 restored the piece to popularity almost until the closure of the theatres in 1642.

If there was a real-life original for Marlowe's Faustus, he appears to have been a self-appointed 'skilled necromancer, astrologer, and friend of magicians' itinerant in Germany in the early sixteenth century, who died in 1540 probably while conducting an experiment with chemicals. The anonymous author of the *Historia von Doktor Johan Fausten*, published in Frankfurt in 1587, seems to have conflated the not very noble, aspiring, or even academic life of this Faustus with medieval legends of a scholar who sold his soul to the Devil. Marlowe derived most of his plot from this prose *Historia*, probably through the fairly close translation into English by a never-identified 'P.F., Gent'. Now generally known as the English *Faustbook*, this translation was published as *The History of the Damnable Life, and Deserved Death of Doctor John Faustus* in 1592.

If Marlowe's play was written earlier than 1592, he would thus have required access to a manuscript copy – although this would not have been unusual in the small and self-regarding literary world of the time. A 'Ballad of Faustus', surviving in the Roxburghe Collection, was licensed for publishing in February 1589, though this may have been prompted by the German *Faustbuch* rather than by Marlowe's play. Ironically, *Doctor Faustus* became popular in Germany and survived there as a puppet-play until the legend was again utilised for 'legitimate' drama by Lessing and Goethe in the later eighteenth century.

The Two Texts of the 'Tragical History'

This edition of *Doctor Faustus* is – and may well remain – unique in the 'Drama Classics' series in including two self-contained texts of the same play. The ways in which the two texts defy being 'the same' have suggested that this might be preferable to opting for one or the other, or trying to conflate the two. To understand how this situation arose, we need to understand something of the Elizabethan attitude to the printing of plays – over which the performing company rather than the author claimed such copyright as it was possible to enforce. We know from Shakespeare's consistent disinterest in the printing of his plays that the existence of a living dramatist was no guarantee of the authority of a printed text: and of Marlowe's output only *Tamburlaine* was published in his own lifetime. Indeed, companies often preferred to keep work unpublished to protect their sole right of performance, and in consequence the early editions of some popular plays appeared in unauthorised or 'pirated' forms.

The earliest edition we have of *Doctor Faustus* is dated 1604 – though this is conjecturally a reprint of a lost edition of 1601, when the play was first entered in the Stationers' Register, to secure its publisher's copyright. The three-year difference was once thought to be crucial, since in 1602 Henslowe's *Diary* records payments to William Birde and Samuel Rowley 'for their adicyones in docter Fostes' – additions which were assumed to have been incorporated into the 1603 and subsequent revivals of the play.

Earlier in the century, therefore, scholars believed that this first extant edition of *Doctor Faustus*, known and printed here as the A-text, was probably closer to Marlowe's original than the edition published in 1616, which is longer by over a third – and has been dubbed, with immaculate logic, the B-text. However, in a monumental work of bibliographical scholarship, *Marlowe's Doctor Faustus, 1604-1616* (Oxford: Clarendon Press, 1950), W.W. Greg demonstrated – it seemed as conclusively as the gaps in our knowledge permitted – that, so far from being an expansion by other writers of the A-text, the 1616 version of the play (the B-text) must already have been in existence when the earlier edition was printed. Greg argued that the A-text was almost certainly a 'memorial reconstruction' – that is, one put together by actors from their recollections of an actual performance, probably, in this case, as cut and adapted for touring purposes.

The differences between the two texts are substantial. The B-text amplifies the scenes at the papal court, and introduces the Emperor's rival nominee for the papacy, Bruno, who is freed by the patriotic Faustus from the Pope's clutches. At the Emperor's palace, an elaborate retaliation is planned by the humiliated Benvolio and is duly thwarted by the omnipotent Faustus. And a great deal is made of the schemings of the cheated Horse-Courser and his companions to get their revenges, all of which are duly frustrated and defeated by Faustus. These episodes add to the comic weight of the play, although it seems likely that their omission from the A-text reflects no nice adjustment of dramatic balance, but rather (as the deletion of various other supernatural and spectacular effects confirms) the need to cut technically complicated scenes from a touring version of the play.

Before Greg's seemingly definitive rethink, most critics had preferred the A-text not just because of its presumed 'authority', but because, of the two, it was clearly the more 'serious'. But if the amplified high-jinks of the B-text represented later additions, might not the comic incidents of the A-text also, as one nineteenth-century editor succinctly put it, be 'expunged with advantage' – or at least passed over in dignified critical silence? Even in 1948 a critic of the stature of Helen Gardner could make passing reference to this 'obviously mutilated' play – while as late as 1969, when the most widely utilised edition of Marlowe's *Complete Plays* was published in the 'Penguin Classics' series, its editor, J.B. Steane, admitted that he had only 'reluctantly' based his version of *Faustus* on the 1616 text, regretting that the 'light, simple-minded comedy . . . distracts the mind from what is serious and valuable in the play'. Even in the A-text, he added sternly, there was 'quite enough knockabout and emptiness in the middle section' already.

The pendulum of critical opinion has continued to swing, notably assisted by the findings of a later textual scholar, Fredson Bowers; and by the 'seventies critical opinion once more favoured Birde and Rowley as mainly responsible for the additions to the B-text, perhaps prompted by Alleyn's planned retirement. Thus, whereas the B-text had been chosen for the edition first published in the magisterial Revels Plays series in 1962, the A-text was preferred for the rival New Mermaid edition of 1989. Then, in 1993, an entirely new Revels edition appeared, on which by permission our own is based – and the decision was taken to include, as do we, the full texts of *both* versions of the play. Bibliographical niceties aside, this appropriately signalled a different focus of controversy – over the varying kinds of 'authority' the two versions might be taken to represent.

So: should we be aiming to reconstruct the text as first conceived by its author – until very recently what Shakespearean scholarship sought so earnestly to 'retrieve'? Or should we actually prefer a version representing the corporate decisions of a theatre company as to what best works on a stage? Or does the only authority lie in the postmodern conception of what constitutes a 'text'? This is now said to be always variable and indeterminate, subject to the changing circumstances, prejudices and needs of each individual 'reader' and to the shifting socio-political context of ever-changing times. Actors and directors might have been forgiven a wry smile at this insight – for their 'performance text', however derived, has always had to be brought to new life, every evening they perform.

The Critics' Views of Faustus' Fortunes

Of *Doctor Faustus*, critics have claimed with equal assurance that, in Leo Kirschbaum's words, 'there is no more obvious Christian document in all Elizabethan drama', or, with Paul Kocher, that it was part of Marlowe's 'unremitting warfare with Christianity'. Generically, it is almost as readily supposed these days to express the pervasive 'comic spirit' discerned by Robert Ornstein as to be the 'tragical history' its title-pages suggest. Indeed, by using textbook criteria, *Faustus* may be pronounced not really a play at all, let alone a tragedy, since nothing, really, *happens*: Faustus learns that he has been in Hell all along, as Mephistopheles told him on their first acquaintance. Like Tamburlaine, he simply runs out of time.

As for Faustus himself, he may be declared either an 'heroic rebel' or the rightfully condemned subject of an 'orthodox Christian sermon'. He may be variously perceived as of the traditional 'aspiring mind', or, in Philip Brockbank's view, as the worthy embodiment of a 'romantic agony between extremities of hope and despair' – or again, through H.W. Matalene's eyes, as 'merely superficial' even in his scholarship, a man who loves 'knowing' but hates 'learning'. Add to this the difference in tone as well as in length between the two texts of the play, and the possibility of an initial collaborator and later 'improvers', and all the ingredients are there for a debate which seems doomed to remain eternally inconclusive.

Nicholas Brooke first presented the view that *all* these contradictory ingredients are present, but in a state of creative tension. It was already a commonplace that *Doctor Faustus* was indebted to the late-medieval tradition of morality plays, in which personified representations of good and evil contend for the soul of an average man – Everyman, Mankind – who is eventually redeemed. Brooke, however, started from the undeniable premise that Faustus is *not* saved, and suggested that – as in each of his plays – Marlowe was conducting an experiment in form. *Faustus*, he concluded, 'used the fullest potential of the morality structure so that the conventional moral idea became untenable'. By this view, it is pointless looking for a 'moral argument' or even for 'character' in Faustus himself: rather, the 'directive intelligence' is 'concerned to explore the ambiguities of the human predicament'.

The problem with this otherwise seductive argument is: how do you act it? We have long since understood the fallacy of Havelock Ellis's assertion that *Faustus* is a 'dramatic poem rather than a regular drama' – not least through the rediscovery of the play in the live theatre which Ellis (as editor of the popular Mermaid edition) helped to bring about. Simply, it *works* on stage – and this may be in part because, however the performance styles of an Alleyn and a Burbage may have differed, those actors and their authors seem to have shared the assumption that Elizabethan audiences had a distinctive and self-consistent way of simultaneously 'listening to' and 'looking at' a play.

From the woodcuts which decorated the verses of their emblem books, to the words of welcome spoken within the triumphal arch of a civic pageant, to the dance of death in Old St. Paul's, all those experiences of Elizabethan Londoners in any way analogous to their theatre-going suggest that they perceived a special kind of complementarity between word and image. For them, *Faustus* would not have been a 'dramatic poem' – or even a tragedy, as Aristotle or the neoclassical critic Castelvetro or Marlowe's near-contemporary Sir Philip Sidney would have defined the form. Rather, it was a verbal scenario for theatrical illustration, whose structure they perceived as deriving from an essentially medieval rather than a classical tradition.

Brooke was right to suggest that it was *against* the grain of the medieval theological tradition that Marlowe was pushing: but no less surely was Marlowe working *within* the frame of the 'comic strip' tradition of medieval art – as played out in stained-glass windows, along Chaucer's tale-strewn road to Canterbury, or in mystery plays trundling one after another through city streets. It is along such an axis that Marlowe's procession of ancient and modern morality figures is plotted – sins and seductresses in anachronistic parade, ringmastered by an existential devil who knows that Hell is all around us. Caught in the middle is Faustus, a proud but confused academic trying to find his way between the worlds these figures portend: comic and tragic, Christian and satanic, heroic and hedonistic.

'The Man that in His Study Sits'

Christopher Marlowe was, like Faustus, 'born of parents of base stock'. The scholarship he therefore needed to go to Cambridge University was renewable after the award of a Bachelor's degree only if the recipient intended to proceed to Holy Orders – as Marlowe must at least officially have intended. But so frequent were his absences during the last two years of his Master's course that the university authorities would have refused him his degree, had they not received an assurance from the Privy Council that he had 'done her Majesty good service'. Conjecturally, this was as a spy in the Catholic seminary at Rheims, where the Jesuits were trained for their task of restoring England to the Catholic fold. Modern scholars, reacting against the earlier tendency to read biographical significance into every facet of Marlowe's work, tend to be wary about suggesting any correspondence between Marlowe in theological disguise among the papists and Faustus in his cloak of invisibility at the papal palace. More important, certainly, is not *where* Marlowe went when he detached himself from his academic studies, but *why*, like Faustus, he chose to abandon them.

One of the Privy Councillors who urged that Marlowe be granted his degree was Sir Francis Walsingham – himself a Cambridge man, and probably Marlowe's spymaster. Another was Burghley, by this time Lord Treasurer – and also Chancellor of the University of Cambridge. Yet another was Archbishop Whitgift, who, back in 1570, as Master of Trinity College, Cambridge, had masterminded the enactment of new statutes designed to curb the powers of the Fellows, some of whom were beginning to display puritan sympathies. Made Vice-Chancellor in the same year, Whitgift even enjoyed the right to imprison members of his own university. Another graduate of Trinity, Edward Coke, was one of Burghley's protégés, and so not entirely disinterested when he described the universities as 'the suns, eyes, and minds of the kingdom, from which religion, liberal education, and sound learning are spread most abundantly to every part of the realm'.

Coke's great rival, and fellow alumnus of Trinity, Sir Francis Bacon, would more probably have agreed with the description of the aims of the universities as summed up by the modern historian Christopher Hill – 'to produce clerics for the state church, and to give a veneer of polite learning to young gentlemen, few of whom had any intention of taking a degree'. The Elizabethan statutes had firmly restored rhetoric, logic, and philosophy as the basis of studies in arts – all as preserved in academic amber by the medieval schoolmen. It was thus no part of a scholar's life to conduct research, still less to pursue new truths – but, precisely as Faustus puts it, to 'live and die in Aristotle's works', which formed the 'set texts' in most subjects.

As J.A. Reynolds has pointed out, Faustus' critique of conventional learning is also close to that of Marlowe's near-contemporary Fulke Greville, who characterised logic as a 'tyranny / of subtile rules, distinctions, terms, and notions' which relied on the 'strained sense of words'. Law was described by Greville as a 'petty case of paltry legacies', while, with Faustus, he recognised the 'proper subject' of medicine as mortality. Yet behind the criticisms of Greville and others such as Bacon and Sir John Davies lay a programme of reform – whereas Faustus' dissatisfaction with his university studies derives from a world view still circumscribed not only by the rigidities of scholasticism, but by the hierarchies and correspondences implicit in the Ptolemaic view of the universe. Faustus *perceives* the limitations of his studies – but proceeds to work within them. He rejects divinity – yet seeks not immortality but a prescribed limit to his own life. He despises the worldly rewards of the law – yet his ambitions hinge only on wealth and power. He knows that medicine cannot confer eternal life – but neither, it appears, can Mephistopheles.

Knowledge, Power and Magic

The scientific historian J. Bronowski dates the modern world from the publication, in 1558, of a book by Giambattista della Porta called *Natural Magic*. By 1620, declares Bronowski, the scientific revolution was complete, with the recognition by Francis Bacon that 'we cannot command nature except by obeying her'. *Faustus* falls midway through this period of adjustment to a new view of the world – and of 'magic'.

It was Bacon who coined the phrase 'knowledge is power' – and *all* knowledge was now legitimised as the proper subject of scientific enquiry. But Descartes had not yet declared the separation of body from soul: and nor was magic yet separable from science, astrology from astronomy, alchemy from chemistry. Napier, who discovered logarithms, believed that the Pope was Antichrist, and earnestly tried to calculate the date when the Apocalypse would fall due. Even that canniest of good housekeepers, the Queen herself, and her astute Lord Chancellor Burghley invested money in Sir Walter Ralegh's expedition of 1595 to discover El Dorado. If inexhaustible gold could not yet be distilled by the alchemists, maybe it could be found in the upper reaches of the Orinoco.

Ralegh himself typified the 'new' man whose pursuit of knowledge embraced both the rational and the occult. He knew, too, the power of the drama, and, as Stephen Greenblatt's *Renaissance Self-Fashioning* reveals, theatricalised his own life to the very end. He called magic 'the wisdom of nature' – 'not the babblings of the Aristotelians, but that which bringeth to light the inmost virtues and draweth them out of nature's hidden bosom to human use'. Ralegh was a patron of John Dee, who, as a Fellow of Trinity College, Cambridge, had staged there a production of Aristophanes' *Peace* with ingenious flying effects as early as 1546. Dee had soon become disenchanted with the limitations of the Cambridge syllabus, and taught instead at Louvain and Paris before returning to England – to make his reputation as an astrologer, consulted on occasion by the Queen herself.

Ralegh's circle included both the occultist Matthew Roydon, and the brilliant mathematician and cartographer Thomas Hariot – who made himself a telescope almost as powerful as Galileo's, with which he was the first to observe Halley's Comet. Yet Hariot was briefly imprisoned after the Gunpowder Plot because he had cast the King's horoscope for one of the suspects, Northumberland – himself known as 'the wizard earl' on account of his dabblings in magic.

It was such men who led the battle in favour of the 'moderns' against the 'ancients', elevating Ramus above Aristotle in dialectics, Paracelsus above Galen in medicine, and Copernicus above Ptolemy in astronomy. In short, they disputed the pre-eminence of all those who had fashioned Faustus' universe – except God himself. Yet if the new philosophy called *all* in doubt, even God could not go unchallenged for long. And the young Christopher Marlowe, himself disparagingly described as 'Ralegh's man', was, of course, in the end suspected of challenging God.

The Queen's favour might protect Ralegh himself, but in 1587 he had been described by Sir Anthony Bagot as 'the best-hated man of the world'. And once Elizabeth was dead, Ralegh gave what proved to be mortal offence to her successor James – not least in his *History of the World*, in which he took every chance to illustrate God's punishment of wicked rulers. The 'divine right' of kings was a relatively recent concept, and all the more dangerous to challenge for that reason. James relished the occasions when he could 'touch' for the King's Evil, scrofula, since the act was emblematic of his own divine authority. 'Touching' was supposed to effect a magical cure: and James it was who had written a treatise on *Demonology* which reflected the ever-increasing interest in the kind of magic which Faustus himself professed – the conjuring of spirits and the worship of the Devil.

The Devil and All His Works

As Jan Kott tells us, the 'pious Lutheran' who wrote the German *Faustbuch* 'borrowed the devil's mock robes' with which Faustus invests Mephistopheles 'from Luther himself'. For it had been the great protestant reformer who, as he sat translating the Scriptures, had seen the Devil dressed as a monk peering over his shoulder. The period in which *Doctor Faustus* reached the stage saw an upsurge of puritanism in England, and the two decades of the 1580s and 1590s also saw 455 of the 790 indictments for witchcraft made during Elizabeth's reign. For protestantism – through its repudiation of the 'superstitious' elements, such as transubstantiation, in Catholic doctrine – left the Devil to perform all the best magic.

Thus, the puritans deplored even the litany as a 'conjuring of God', and the very word 'conjuror' came at this time to denote a Catholic priest – while the Catholic Church was the source of 'all wicked sorcery', a list duly being drawn up of eighteen popes who had been conjurors or sorcerers. So when Faustus plays tricks on the Pope, in protestant eyes he would have been turning the Pope's own weapons against him. If the Pope was Antichrist, there could certainly be no such thing as 'good' conjuring: so folk cures and blessings which, because they were reinforced by Christian prayer, had been over-looked by officialdom before the Reformation, were now condemned as superstitious along with the rituals from which they derived.

In a population of somewhere between four and five million, the Spanish ambassador estimated in 1617 that there were 900,000 atheists in England. This was a prejudiced estimate, no doubt – but with it we may compare the Pope's no less prejudiced estimate that there remained but 100,000 adherents to the Catholic faith, and the more objective view of the modern historian Lawrence Stone that the Elizabethan period was 'the age of greatest religious indifference before the twentieth century'. It was ironic that, in this superstitious yet sceptical age, scepticism would have been enough to brand a man an atheist – as were Marlowe himself, Ralegh, Hariot, the Earl of Oxford, and many another English intellectual.

John Dee's friend and fellow alchemist Edward Kelly is among those enumerated by the historian Keith Thomas as having denied the divinity of Christ – but no less reprehensible was it, in terms of the function of religion as a sanction, to deny the existence of the Devil. When, in 1573, a group of sectaries in the diocese of Ely asserted that the idea of Hell was purely allegorical, they were not only ques-tioning the threat of punishment in the next life, but removing one of the strongest inducements to good behaviour in this.

Keith Thomas also points out that in the 'widely influential Great Catechism by the sixteenth-century Jesuit, Peter Cansius, the name of Christ appeared sixty-three times, that of Satan sixty-seven'. While Catholics believed that Luther had been converted to protestantism by Satan, puritan iconoclasts saw even 'an image of Christ in the rood-loft as a picture of the Devil'. And *Doctor Faustus* is not just existen-tially up to date in having Mephistopheles declare that Hell is all about us, but very much of its own times in recognising the *personal* pervasiveness of Satan himself.

In cases of 'possession', people, interestingly, drew on their theatrical memories to evoke the experience, as when a 'possessed' person in 1573 was said to have been 'monstrously transformed . . . much like the picture of the Devil in a play'. And the martyrologist John Foxe is said to have cured a case of possession in 1574 in which the victim was assailed by a combination of threats and promises much like those with which Mephistopheles tempts Faustus, including a cupboard full of plate and a 'painted woman' to enjoy. Foxe eventually outwitted Satan in what appears to have resembled a formal disputation: the Devil, too, had evidently received an academic education.

Pride, Despair, and Contract Theology

The search of the alchemists was not only for the philosopher's stone but for the *quinta essentia* which would bestow eternal life: and it has seemed curious to some critics that Faustus – unlike the romantic Faust created by Goethe, who wants eternal youth – makes no demands for the extension of his physical existence beyond a normal span. However, to a contemporary of Marlowe's, the surprising thing about Faustus' bargain might not have been that its rewards were so trivial but that they were, by the usual standards, so impressive. Most witches who confessed, genuinely or otherwise, to having made pacts with the Devil did so in exchange for little more than an assurance that they would never want for food or clothing. Faustus' must have been a 'glorious' soul indeed to merit such a commitment of Mephistopheles' time.

The textual scholar W.W. Greg, confessing his amateur status as a literary critic, put forward the view that Faustus was irredeemably damned only after he had enjoyed sexual congress with the succuba of Helen of Troy. Greg also wondered whether it would be 'idle to speculate how far the "atheist" Marlowe, whom gossip accused of what we call "unnatural" vice, may have dwelt in imagination on the direst sin of which human flesh is capable'. Even the wretched informer Baines did not accuse Marlowe of demoniality: but Greg's suggestion does have the merit of deriving from what *happens* in the play, not from an arbitrary prescription – ironically, derived from

Aristotle's view of tragedy – that Faustus must manifest some 'tragic flaw'. Ambition, curiosity, and pride have variously been proposed – as has despair, understood as the converse of pride, if Faustus believes God to be incapable of forgiving such overweening pride as his, and *therefore* despairs.

Even those critics who acknowledge a simpler cause of Faustus' downfall – that he has signed a contract with the Devil – tend to concern themselves only with the theological niceties of the pact: whether Faustus, if he has indeed become a 'spirit in form and substance', is from that moment inescapably the Devil's own, or whether folklore and common law agree that a contract with the Devil is unenforcable and void. This is to ignore what we might call the Shylock factor: an Elizabethan audience's *assumption* that a contract is legally binding, whether commercially or as a theatrical 'given'. And so far from subordinating legal to theological considerations, some puritans of the time appear to have been doing the reverse – in their development of what the historian Christopher Hill has called 'contract theology', which led, for example, to the use of *covenants* between certain congregations and their ministers.

This produced so strong a sense of the sanctity of contracts that, as Horatio Palavicino explained to a patron in 1593, it transcended any other kind of loyalty – and even came 'near to suggesting that a bargain could be struck with God, and that he could be held to the letter of his bond'. This would fit perfectly with Lucifer's claim to Faustus that 'Christ cannot save thy soul, for he is just. / There's none but I have interest in the same.' God, in short, is himself bound by contract law to give the Devil his due. And however theologically offensive this may seem, what counts is an *audience's* perception of its validity.

Faustus makes his contract for a specific period: twenty-four years. For him, time simply runs out. And time, during the Renaissance, was ceasing to be measured through the recurrent turning of the seasons, with its pattern of saints' days and festivities and fasts. Such a cyclical sense of time can still be found in Shakespeare, but there is no trace of it in *Doctor Faustus*, in which time flows in an inexorable and undeviating line – just as the puritans, in Stephen Greenblatt's words, would have liked to see time altogether 'flattened out', into an inexorable flow of six days' labour and one day's rest.

No less significantly, protestantism had also eliminated purgatory – that half-way house between terrestrial and eternal time, where a finite period of suffering might expiate one's sins. Faustus, home to die in protestant Wittenberg (where Hamlet learned to doubt the purgatory whence comes his father's ghost), knows he cannot 'live in Hell a thousand years, / A hundred thousand, and at last be saved.' Punishment, like paradise, is forever.

Faustus and the Pleasure Principle

Many critics have remarked that Faustus' quotations from Jerome's Bible are incomplete, threatening damnation while ignoring the hope of redemption. Besides his Bible, Faustus knows well the works of Aristotle, of Galen – and of Justinian, the Byzantine emperor who codified what was still known and taught as 'Roman law'. And his quotations from Justinian, here translated, are also unfinished: 'If one thing is willed to two persons, one of them shall have the thing itself, the other the value of the thing. . .', and 'A father cannot disinherit his son unless. . .'. Faustus is disinherited from his heavenly father *because* he relinquishes 'the thing itself', his immortal soul, in return for his own estimate of 'the value of the thing' – twenty-four years of earthly profit and delight.

In his 1986 study of Marlowe, Simon Shepherd pointed out the paradox of Faustus' quest for pleasure, as summed up by the French philosopher Jean Bodin as early as 1566: 'Because nature has engendered first in every being the desire for self-preservation, the earliest activities of man are related to things impossible to forgo. Later they are directed to matters without which we can, indeed, live, but not at all comfortably; or if comfortably, not splendidly; or if splendidly, still not with that keen joy which delights the senses most sweetly. Hence the desire to acquire riches.' But the implication is and remains clear: ultimate pleasure remains forever beyond reach.

Protestantism recognised this paradox, too. It legitimised the pursuit of profit as an implicit sign of grace – it was Calvin who finally lifted the ages-old and now largely theoretical ban on usury – but found itself uncomfortable before the prospect of pleasure as a concomitant of profit. Hence the virtue the puritans made of *delayed* gratification, a corollary of what Freud's contemporary Max Weber labelled the 'protestant work ethic'.

Marlowe's Faustus remains a work-centered protestant even in that voluptuous dalliance by which Greg was so fascinated and repelled. He seeks not so much pleasure as power – and power as *energy* rather than dominion. What he responds to in Helen is not so much her beauty as its capacity for energising men into building a fleet of ships with which to besiege and destroy a city, or to confer immortality with a kiss. Unlike the romantic Goethe, Marlowe allows Faustus no relationship with a flesh-and-blood Marguerite, nor does this Helen, as in the *Faustbook*, give birth to a succubus-boy. Despite Greenblatt's observation that 'the family is at the centre of most Elizabethan and Jacobean drama as it is at the centre of the period's economic structure', Faustus has no family or even wife – only, it appears, a choice between his studies and the illicit pursuit of pleasure.

He does not return home to die: he returns to his office, where he should have been working away all this time, confident of the ultimate form of delayed gratification, the salvation of his soul. Instead, he has exchanged twenty-four years of profit and delight for delayed damnation, an eternity in Hell.

Simon Trussler

For Further Reading

Marlowe has been the subject of many biographies, of which *In Search of Christopher Marlowe*, by A.D. Wraight (London: Macdonald, 1965), is probably the most accessible and widest-ranging. Those wishing to follow the critical debate over his work will find earlier comments assembled in *Marlowe: the Critical Heritage, 1588-1896*, edited by Millar MacLure (London: Routledge, 1979). Modern opinions are collected in Judith O'Neill's *Critics on Marlowe* (University of Miami Press, 1970); Brian Morris's *Christopher Marlowe* in the 'Mermaid Critical Commentaries' series (London: Benn, 1968); and Clifford Leech's *Marlowe: a Collection of Critical Essays* in the 'Twentieth-Century Views' series (Englewood Cliffs: Prentice-Hall, 1964).

John Jump's *Marlowe: Doctor Faustus* in the 'Casebook' series (London: Macmillan, 1969) offers a selection of criticism on that play, on which more extensive commentaries and annotation can be found in the editions in the 'Revels Plays' series, edited by David Bevington and Eric Rasmussen (Manchester University Press, 1993), and the 'New Mermaid' series, edited by Roma Gill (London: Black, 1989). Marlowe's other plays may be conveniently read in the collected editions in the Penguin Classics series, edited by J.B. Steane (Harmondsworth: Penguin, 1969), and the World's Classics series, edited by David Bevington and Eric Rasmussen (Oxford University Press, 1995).

Marlowe: Key Dates

1564   6 Feb., born, son of John Marlowe, a shoemaker.

1579   Jan., received one of the church scholarships for 'fifty poor boys' to King's School, Canterbury.

1580   Dec., entered Corpus Christi College, Cambridge, on a six-year scholarship intended to lead to Holy Orders.

1584   Awarded his BA Degree.

1586   Conjectural date of his tragedy *Dido, Queen of Carthage*, based on Virgil's *Aeneid*.

1587   Rumoured to have joined the Catholic seminary at Rheims, but awarded his MA Degree from Cambridge in July. Both parts of *Tamburlaine the Great* (published 1590) were probably performed late in the year by the Admiral's Men.

1588   Conjectural date of performance of *Doctor Faustus* by Admiral's Men – alternatively by Pembroke's Men, 1592 or 1593.

1589   Probable first performance of *The Jew of Malta* (published under Thomas Heywood's supervision, 1633) by Strange's Men.

1592   Probable first performance of the history play *Edward II* (published 1594) by Pembroke's Men, touring the provinces during a plague closure of the London theatres. Employed as a government messenger during siege of Rouen. *The Massacre of Paris* (published *c.* 1600) first performed around this time.

1593   20 May, examined before the Privy Council, but released on bail. 30 May, stabbed to death by Ingram Frizer. 1 June, buried in an unmarked grave in the Deptford parish church of St. Nicholas. Posthumous publication of his translation of *All Ovid's Elegies* (1595), the sensual epic poem *Hero and Leander* (1598), and *Lucan's First Book* in translation (1600).

DOCTOR FAUSTUS: A-TEXT

Dramatis Personae

THE CHORUS.
DOCTOR JOHN FAUSTUS.
WAGNER.
GOOD ANGEL.
EVIL ANGEL.
VALDES.
CORNELIUS.
THREE SCHOLARS.
MEPHISTOPHELES.
ROBIN, *the Clown.*
DEVILS.
RAFE.
LUCIFER.
BEELZEBUB.
PRIDE,
COVETOUSNESS,
WRATH,
ENVY,
GLUTTONY,
SLOTH,
LECHERY,
   the Seven Deadly Sins.

THE POPE.
THE CARDINAL OF
   LORRAINE.
FRIARS.
A VINTNER.
THE EMPEROR OF
   GERMANY, CHARLES V.
A KNIGHT.
ATTENDANTS.
ALEXANDER THE GREAT,
HIS PARAMOUR,
   spirits.
A HORSE-COURSER.
THE DUKE OF VANHOLT.
THE DUCHESS OF
   VANHOLT.
HELEN OF TROY, *a spirit.*
AN OLD MAN.

[Prologue]

Enter CHORUS.

CHORUS. Not marching now in fields of Trasimene
    Where Mars did mate the Carthaginians,
    Nor sporting in the dalliance of love
    In courts of kings where state is overturned,
    Nor in the pomp of proud audacious deeds,   5
    Intends our muse to daunt his heavenly verse.
    Only this, gentlemen: we must perform
    The form of Faustus' fortunes, good or bad.
    To patient judgements we appeal our plaud,
    And speak for Faustus in his infancy.   10
    Now is he born, his parents base of stock,
    In Germany, within a town called Rhode.
    Of riper years to Wittenberg he went,
    Whereas his kinsmen chiefly brought him up.
    So soon he profits in divinity,   15
    The fruitful plot of scholarism graced,
    That shortly he was graced with doctor's name,
    Excelling all whose sweet delight disputes
    In heavenly matters of theology;
    Till, swoll'n with cunning of a self-conceit,   20
    His waxen wings did mount above his reach,
    And melting heavens conspired his overthrow.
    For, falling to a devilish exercise,
    And glutted more with learning's golden gifts,
    He surfeits upon cursèd necromancy;   25
    Nothing so sweet as magic is to him,
    Which he prefers before his chiefest bliss.
    And this the man that in his study sits.

    Exit.

Act I

[I.i]

Enter FAUSTUS *in his study.*

FAUSTUS. Settle thy studies, Faustus, and begin
    To sound the depth of that thou wilt profess.
    Having commenced, be a divine in show,
    Yet level at the end of every art,
    And live and die in Aristotle's works.   5
    Sweet *Analytics*, 'tis thou hast ravished me!
    [*He reads.*] *Bene disserere est finis logices.*
    Is to dispute well logic's chiefest end?
    Affords this art no greater miracle?
    Then read no more; thou hast attained the end.   10
    A greater subject fitteth Faustus' wit.
    Bid *On kai me on* farewell. Galen, come!
    Seeing *ubi desinit philosophus, ibi incipit medicus,*
    Be a physician, Faustus. Heap up gold,
    And be eternised for some wondrous cure.   15
    [*He reads.*] *Summum bonum medicinae sanitas:*
    The end of physic is our body's health.
    Why Faustus, hast thou not attained that end?
    Is not thy common talk sound aphorisms?
    Are not thy bills hung up as monuments,   20
    Whereby whole cities have escaped the plague
    And thousand desp'rate maladies been eased?
    Yet art thou still but Faustus, and a man.
    Wouldst thou make man to live eternally?
    Or, being dead, raise them to life again?   25
    Then this profession were to be esteemed.
    Physic, farewell! Where is Justinian?
    [*He reads.*] *Si una eademque res legatur duobus,*
    Alter rem, alter valorem rei, etc.

A pretty case of paltry legacies!   30
[*He reads.*] *Exhaereditare filium non potest pater nisi* –
Such is the subject of the Institute
And universal body of the Church
His study fits a mercenary drudge
Who aims at nothing but external trash –   35
Too servile and illiberal for me.
When all is done, divinity is best.
Jerome's Bible, Faustus, view it well.
[*He reads.*] *Stipendium peccati mors est.* Ha!
Stipendium, etc.   40
The reward of sin is death. That's hard.
[*He reads.*] *Si peccasse negamus, fallimur
Et nulla est in nobis veritas.*
If we say that we have no sin,
We deceive ourselves, and there's no truth in us.   45
Why then belike we must sin,
And so consequently die.
Ay, we must die an everlasting death.
What doctrine call you this, *Che serà, serà,*
What will be, shall be? Divinity, adieu!   50

[*He picks up a book of magic.*]

These metaphysics of magicians
And necromantic books are heavenly,
Lines, circles, signs, letters, and characters –
Ay, these are those that Faustus most desires.
O, what a world of profit and delight,   55
Of power, of honour, of omnipotence,
Is promised to the studious artisan!
All things that move between the quiet poles
Shall be at my comrnand. Emperors and kings
Are but obeyed in their several provinces,   60
Nor can they raise the wind or rend the clouds;
But his dominion that exceeds in this
Stretcheth as far as doth the mind of man
A sound magician is a mighty god.
Here, Faustus, try thy brains to gain a deity.   65
Wagner!

Enter WAGNER.

     Commend me to my dearest friends,
  The German Valdes and Cornelius.
  Request them earnestly to visit me.

WAGNER. I will, sir.

 Exit.

FAUSTUS. Their conference will be a greater help to me 70
  Than all my labours, plod I ne'er so fast.

 Enter the GOOD ANGEL *and the* EVIL ANGEL.

GOOD ANGEL. O Faustus, lay that damnèd book aside
  And gaze not on it, lest it tempt thy soul
  And heap God's heavy wrath upon thy head!
  Read, read the Scriptures. That is blasphemy. 75

EVIL ANGEL. Go forward, Faustus, in that famous art
  Wherein all nature's treasury is contained.
  Be thou on earth as Jove is in the sky,
  Lord and commander of these elements.

 Exeunt [ANGELS].

FAUSTUS. How am I glutted with conceit of this! 80
  Shall I make spirits fetch me what I please,
  Resolve me of all ambiguities,
  Perform what desperate enterprise I will?
  I'll have them fly to India for gold,
  Ransack the ocean for orient pearl, 85
  And search all corners of the new-found world
  For pleasant fruits and princely delicates.
  I'll have them read me strange philosophy
  And tell the secrets of all foreign kings.
  I'll have them wall all Germany with brass 90
  And make swift Rhine circle fair Wittenberg.
  I'll have them fill the public schools with silk,
  Wherewith the students shall be bravely clad.
  I'll levy soldiers with the coin they bring
  And chase the Prince of Parma from our land, 95
  And reign sole king of all our provinces;

Yea, stranger engines for the brunt of war
Than was the fiery keel at Antwerp's bridge
I'll make my servile spirits to invent.
Come, German Valdes and Cornelius,   100
And make me blest with your sage conference!

Enter VALDES *and* CORNELIUS.

Valdes, sweet Valdes, and Cornelius,
Know that your words have won me at the last
To practise magic and concealèd arts.
Yet not your words only, but mine own fantasy,   105
That will receive no object, for my head
But ruminates on necromantic skill.
Philosophy is odious and obscure;
Both law and physic are for petty wits;
Divinity is basest of the three,   110
Unpleasant, harsh, contemptible, and vile.
'Tis magic, magic that hath ravished me.
Then, gentle friends, aid me in this attempt,
And I, that have with concise syllogisms
Gravelled the pastors of the German Church   115
And made the flow'ring pride of Wittenberg
Swarm to my problems as the infernal spirits
On sweet Musaeus when he came to hell,
Will be as cunning as Agrippa was,
Whose shadows made all Europe honour him.   120

VALDES. Faustus, these books, thy wit, and our experience
Shall make all nations to canonise us.
As Indian Moors obey their Spanish lords,
So shall the subjects of every element
Be always serviceable to us three.   125
Like lions shall they guard us when we please,
Like Almaine rutters with their horsemen's staves,
Or Lapland giants, trotting by our sides;
Sometimes like women, or unwedded maids,
Shadowing more beauty in their airy brows   130
Than in the white breasts of the Queen of Love.
From Venice shall they drag huge argosies,
And from America the golden fleece

That yearly stuffs old Philip's treasury,
If learnèd Faustus will be resolute.   135

FAUSTUS. Valdes, as resolute am I in this
As thou to live. Therefore object it not.

CORNELIUS. The miracles that magic will perform
Will make thee vow to study nothing else.
He that is grounded in astrology,   140
Enriched with tongues, well seen in minerals,
Hath all the principles magic doth require.
Then doubt not, Faustus, but to be renowned
And more frequented for this mystery
Than heretofore the Delphian oracle.   145
The spirits tell me they can dry the sea
And fetch the treasure of all foreign wrecks –
Ay, all the wealth that our forefathers hid
Within the massy entrails of the earth.
Then tell me, Faustus, what shall we three want?   150

FAUSTUS. Nothing, Cornelius. O, this cheers my soul!
Come, show me some demonstrations magical,
That I may conjure in some lusty grove
And have these joys in full possession.

VALDES. Then haste thee to some solitary grove,   155
And bear wise Bacon's and Albanus' works,
The Hebrew Psalter, and New Testament;
And whatsoever else is requisite
We will inform thee ere our conference cease.

CORNELIUS. Valdes, first let him know the words of art, 160
And then, all other ceremonies learned,
Faustus may try his cunning by himself.

VALDES. First I'll instruct thee in the rudiments,
And then wilt thou be perfecter than I.

FAUSTUS. Then come and dine with me, and after meat   165
We'll canvass every quiddity thereof,
For ere I sleep I'll try what I can do.
This night I'll conjure, though I die therefore.

Exeunt.

[I.ii]

Enter two SCHOLARS.

FIRST SCHOLAR. I wonder what's become of Faustus, that was
    wont to make our schools ring with '*sic probo*'.

SECOND SCHOLAR. That shall we know, for see, here comes
    his boy.

    Enter WAGNER, [*carrying wine*].

FIRST SCHOLAR. How now, sirrah, where's thy master?   5

WAGNER. God in heaven knows.

SECOND SCHOLAR. Why, dost not thou know?

WAGNER. Yes, I know, but that follows not.

FIRST SCHOLAR. Go to, sirrah! Leave your jesting, and tell
    us where he is.   10

WAGNER. That follows not necessary by force of argument
    that you, being licentiate, should stand upon't. Therefore,
    acknowledge your error, and be attentive.

SECOND SCHOLAR. Why, didst thou not say thou knew'st?

WAGNER. Have you any witness on 't?   15

FIRST SCHOLAR. Yes, sirrah, I heard you.

WAGNER. Ask my fellow if I be a thief.

SECOND SCHOLAR. Well, you will not tell us.

WAGNER. Yes, sir, I will tell you. Yet if you were not dunces,
    you would never ask me such a question. For is not he   20
    corpus naturale? And is not that *mobile*? Then, wherefore
    should you ask me such a question? But that I am by
    nature phlegmatic, slow to wrath, and prone to lechery –
    to love, I would say – it were not for you to come within
    forty foot of the place of execution, although I do not   25
    doubt to see you both hanged the next sessions. Thus,
    having triumphed over you, I will set my countenance
    like a precisian and begin to speak thus: Truly, my dear
    brethren, my master is within at dinner with Valdes and

Cornelius, as this wine, if it could speak, it would inform   30
your worships. And so the Lord bless you, preserve you,
and keep you, my dear brethren, my dear brethren.

Exit.

FIRST SCHOLAR. Nay, then, I fear he is fall'n into that damned
art for which they two are infamous through the world.

SECOND SCHOLAR. Were he a stranger, and not allied to   35
me, yet should I grieve for him. But come, let us go and inform
the Rector, and see if he, by his grave counsel, can reclaim
him.

FIRST SCHOLAR. O, but I fear me nothing can reclaim him.

SECOND SCHOLAR. Yet let us try what we can do.   40

Exeunt.

[I.iii]

Enter FAUSTUS *to conjure, [holding a book].*

FAUSTUS. Now that the gloomy shadow of the earth,
          Longing to view Orion's drizzling look,
          Leaps from th' Antarctic world unto the sky
          And dims the welkin with her pitchy breath,
          Faustus, begin thine incantations,   5
          And try if devils will obey thy hest,
          Seeing thou hast prayed and sacrificed to them.

          [*He draws a circle.*]

          Within this circle is Jehovah's name,
          Forward and backward anagrammatised,
          The breviated names of holy saints,   10
          Figures of every adjunct to the heavens,
          And characters of signs and erring stars,
          By which the spirits are enforced to rise.
          Then fear not, Faustus, but be resolute,
          And try the uttermost magic can perform.   15

Sint mihi dei Acherontis propitii! Valeat numen triplex
Jehovae! Ignei, aerii, aquatici, terreni, spiritus, salvete!
Orientis princeps Lucifer, Beelzebub, inferni ardentis
monarcha, et Demogorgon, propitiamus vos, ut appareat
et surgat Mephistopheles! Quid tu moraris? Per Jehovam,   20
Gehennam, et consecratam aquam quam nunc spargo,
signumque crucis quod nunc facio, et per vota nostra, ipse
nunc surgat nobis dicatus Mephistopheles!

[FAUSTUS *sprinkles holy water and makes a sign of the cross.*]

Enter a Devil [MEPHISTOPHELES].

I charge thee to return and change thy shape.
Thou art too ugly to attend on me.   25
Go, and return an old Franciscan friar;
That holy shape becomes a devil best.

Exit Devil [MEPHISTOPHELES].

I see there's virtue in my heavenly words.
Who would not be proficient in this art?
How pliant is this Mephistopheles,   30
Full of obedience and humility!
Such is the force of magic and my spells.
Now, Faustus, thou art conjurer laureate,
That canst command great Mephistopheles.
Quin redis, Mephistopheles, fratris imagine!   35

Enter MEPHISTOPHELES [*disguised as a friar*].

MEPHISTOPHELES. Now, Faustus, what wouldst thou have me do?

FAUSTUS. I charge thee wait upon me whilst I live,
    To do whatever Faustus shall command,
    Be it to make the moon drop from her sphere
    Or the ocean to overwhelm the world.   40

MEPHISTOPHELES. I am a servant to great Lucifer
    And may not follow thee without his leave.
    No more than he commands must we perform.

FAUSTUS. Did not he charge thee to appear to me?`   44

MEPHISTOPHELES. No, I came now hither of mine own accord.

FAUSTUS. Did not my conjuring speeches raise thee? Speak.

MEPHISTOPHELES. That was the cause, but yet *per accidens*.
    For when we hear one rack the name of God,
    Abjure the Scriptures and his Saviour Christ,
    We fly in hope to get his glorious soul,   50
    Nor will we come unless he use such means
    Whereby he is in danger to be damned.
    Therefore, the shortest cut for conjuring
    Is stoutly to abjure the Trinity
    And pray devoutly to the prince of hell.   55

FAUSTUS. So Faustus hath
    Already done, and holds this principle:
    There is no chief but only Beelzebub,
    To whom Faustus doth dedicate himself.
    This word 'damnation' terrifies not him,   60
    For he confounds hell in Elysium.
    His ghost be with the old philosophers!
    But leaving these vain trifles of men's souls,
    Tell me what is that Lucifer thy lord?   64

MEPHISTOPHELES. Arch-regent and commander of all spirits.

FAUSTUS. Was not that Lucifer an angel once?

MEPHISTOPHELES. Yes, Faustus, and most dearly loved of God.

FAUSTUS. How comes it then that he is prince of devils?

MEPHISTOPHELES. O, by aspiring pride and insolence,
    For which God threw him from the face of heaven.   70

FAUSTUS. And what are you that live with Lucifer?

MEPHISTOPHELES. Unhappy spirits that fell with Lucifer,
    Conspired against our God with Lucifer,
    And are for ever damned with Lucifer.

FAUSTUS. Where are you damned?   75

MEPHISTOPHELES. In hell.

FAUSTUS. How comes it then that thou art out of hell?

MEPHISTOPHELES. Why, this is hell, nor am I out of it.

Think'st thou that I, who saw the face of God
And tasted the eternal joys of heaven,   80
Am not tormented with ten thousand hells
In being deprived of everlasting bliss?
O Faustus, leave these frivolous demands,
Which strike a terror to my fainting soul!

FAUSTUS. What, is great Mephistopheles so passionate   85
For being deprivèd of the joys of heaven?
Learn thou of Faustus manly fortitude,
And scorn those joys thou never shalt possess.
Go bear these tidings to great Lucifer:
Seeing Faustus hath incurred eternal death   90
By desp'rate thoughts against Jove's deity,
Say he surrenders up to him his soul,
So he will spare him four-and-twenty years,
Letting him live in all voluptuousness,
Having thee ever to attend on me,   95
To give me whatsoever I shall ask,
To tell me whatsoever I demand,
To slay mine enemies and aid my friends,
And always be obedient to my will.
Go and return to mighty Lucifer,   100
And meet me in my study at midnight,
And then resolve me of thy master's mind.

MEPHISTOPHELES. I will, Faustus.

Exit.

FAUSTUS. Had I as many souls as there be stars,
I'd give them all for Mephistopheles.   105
By him I'll be great emperor of the world
And make a bridge through the moving air
To pass the ocean with a band of men;
I'll join the hills that bind the Afric shore
And make that land continent to Spain,   110
And both contributory to my crown.
The Emp'ror shall not live but by my leave,
Nor any potentate of Germany.
Now that I have obtained what I desire,

I'll live in speculation of this art   115
Till Mephistopheles return again.

Exit.

[I.iv]

Enter WAGNER *and* [ROBIN] *the* CLOWN.

WAGNER. Sirrah boy, come hither.

ROBIN. How, 'boy'? 'Swounds, 'boy'! I hope you have seen
    many boys with such pickedevants as I have. 'Boy',
    quotha?

WAGNER. Tell me, sirrah, hast thou any comings in?   5

ROBIN. Ay, and goings out too, you may see else.

WAGNER. Alas, poor slave, see how poverty jesteth in his
    nakedness! The villain is bare and out of service, and so
    hungry that I know he would give his soul to the devil for
    a shoulder of mutton, though it were blood raw.   10

ROBIN. How? My soul to the devil for a shoulder of mutton,
    though 'twere blood raw? Not so, good friend. By'r Lady,
    I had need have it well roasted, and good sauce to it, if I pay
    so dear.

WAGNER. Well, wilt thou serve me, and I'll make thee go like   15
    Qui mihi discipulus?

ROBIN. How, in verse?

WAGNER. No, sirrah, in beaten silk and stavesacre.

ROBIN. How, how, knave's acre? [*Aside.*] Aye, I thought that
    was all the land his father left him. [*To* WAGNER.] Do ye   20
    hear? I would be sorry to rob you of your living.

WAGNER. Sirrah, I say in stavesacre.

ROBIN. Oho, oho, 'stavesacre'! Why then, belike, if I were your
    man, I should be full of vermin.

WAGNER. So thou shalt, whether thou beest with me or no.   25
     But sirrah, leave your jesting, and bind yourself presently
     unto me for seven years, or I'll turn all the lice about thee
     into familiars, and they shall tear thee in pieces.

ROBIN. Do you hear, sir? You may save that labour. They are   30
     too familiar with me already. 'Swounds, they are as bold
     with my flesh as if they had paid for my meat and drink.

WAGNER. Well, do you hear, sirrah? Hold, take these guilders.

     [*Offering money.*]

ROBIN. Gridirons? What be they?

WAGNER. Why, French crowns.

ROBIN. Mass, but for the name of French crowns a man were   35
     as good have as many English counters. And what should
     I do with these?

WAGNER. Why now, sirrah, thou art at an hour's warning
     whensoever or wheresoever the devil shall fetch thee.

ROBIN. No, no, here, take your gridirons again.   40

     [*He attempts to return the money.*]

WAGNER. Truly, I'll none of them.

ROBIN. Truly, but you shall.

WAGNER [*to the audience*]. Bear witness I gave them him.

ROBIN. Bear witness I give them you again.

WAGNER. Well, I will cause two devils presently to fetch thee   45
     away. – Balioll and Belcher!

ROBIN. Let your Balio and your Belcher come here and I'll
     knock them. They were never so knocked since they were
     devils. Say I should kill one of them, what would folks
     say? 'Do ye see yonder tall fellow in the round slop? He   50
     has killed the devil.' So I should be called 'Kill devil' all
     the parish over.

     Enter two DEVILS, *and* [ROBIN] *the* CLOWN *runs up and
     down crying.*

WAGNER. Balioll and Belcher! Spirits, away!

Exeunt [DEVILS].

ROBIN. What, are they gone? A vengeance on them! They
have vile long nails. There was a he devil and a she devil.   55
I'll tell you how you shall know them: all he devils has horns,
and all she devils has clefts and cloven feet.

WAGNER. Well, sirrah, follow me.

ROBIN. But do you hear? If I should serve you, would you
teach me to raise up Banios and Belcheos?   60

WAGNER. I will teach thee to turn thyself to anything, to a dog,
or a cat, or a mouse, or a rat, or anything.

ROBIN. How? A Christian fellow to a dog or a cat, a mouse or
a rat? No, no, sir. If you turn me into anything, let it be in
the likeness of a little, pretty, frisking flea, that I may be   65
here and there and everywhere. O, I'll tickle the pretty
wenches' plackets! I'll be amongst them, i' faith!

WAGNER. Well, sirrah, come.

ROBIN. But do you hear, Wagner?

WAGNER. How? – Balioll and Belcher!   70

ROBIN. O Lord, I pray sir, let Banio and Belcher go sleep.

WAGNER. Villain, call me Master Wagner, and let thy left eye
be diametarily fixed upon my right heel, with *quasi vestigiis
nostris insistere*.

Exit.

ROBIN. God forgive me, he speaks Dutch fustian. Well, I'll   75
follow him, I'll serve him, that's flat.

Exit.

Act II

[II.i]

Enter FAUSTUS *in his study.*

FAUSTUS. Now, Faustus, must thou needs be damned,
    And canst thou not be saved.
    What boots it then to think of God or heaven?
    Away with such vain fancies and despair!
    Despair in God and trust in Beelzebub. 5
    Now go not backward. No, Faustus, be resolute.
    Why waverest thou? O, something soundeth in mine ears:
    'Abjure this magic, turn to God again!'
    Ay, and Faustus will turn to God again.
    To God? He loves thee not. 10
    The god thou servest is thine own appetite,
    Wherein is fixed the love of Beelzebub.
    To him I'll build an altar and a church,
    And offer lukewarm blood of new-born babes.

    Enter GOOD ANGEL *and* EVIL [ANGEL].

GOOD ANGEL. Sweet Faustus, leave that execrable art. 15

FAUSTUS. Contrition, prayer, repentance – what of them?

GOOD ANGEL. O, they are means to bring thee unto heaven.

EVIL ANGEL. Rather illusions, fruits of lunacy,
    That makes men foolish that do trust them most.

GOOD ANGEL. Sweet Faustus, think of heaven and heavenly
      things. 20

EVIL ANGEL. No, Faustus, think of honour and wealth.

    Exeunt [ANGELS].

FAUSTUS. Of wealth?

Why, the seigniory of Emden shall be mine.
When Mephistopheles shall stand by me,
What god can hurt thee, Faustus? Thou art safe;   25
Cast no more doubts. Come, Mephistopheles,
And bring glad tidings from great Lucifer.
Is't not midnight? Come, Mephistopheles!
Veni, veni, Mephistophile!

Enter MEPHISTOPHELES.

Now tell, what says Lucifer thy lord?   30

MEPHISTOPHELES. That I shall wait on Faustus whilst he lives,
So he will buy my service with his soul.

FAUSTUS. Already Faustus hath hazarded that for thee.

MEPHISTOPHELES. But, Faustus, thou must bequeath it solemnly
And write a deed of gift with thine own blood,   35
For that security craves great Lucifer.
If thou deny it, I will back to hell.

FAUSTUS. Stay, Mephistopheles, and tell me, what good will my
soul do thy lord?

MEPHISTOPHELES. Enlarge his kingdom.   40

FAUSTUS. Is that the reason he tempts us thus?

MEPHISTOPHELES. *Solamen miseris socios habuisse doloris.*

FAUSTUS. Have you any pain, that tortures others?

MEPHISTOPHELES. As great as have the human souls of men.
But tell me, Faustus, shall I have thy soul?   45
And I will be thy slave, and wait on thee,
And give thee more than thou hast wit to ask.

FAUSTUS. Ay, Mephistopheles, I give it thee.

MEPHISTOPHELES. Then stab thine arm courageously,
And bind thy soul that at some certain day   50
Great Lucifer may claim it as his own,
And then be thou as great as Lucifer.

FAUSTUS [*cutting his arm*]. Lo, Mephistopheles, for love of thee
I cut mine arm, and with my proper blood

Assure my soul to be great Lucifer's,   55
Chief lord and regent of perpetual night.
View here the blood that trickles from mine arm,
And let it be propitious for my wish.

MEPHISTOPHELES. But Faustus, thou must write it in
    manner of a deed of gift.   60

FAUSTUS. Ay, so I will. [*He writes.*] But Mephistopheles,
    My blood congeals, and I can write no more.

MEPHISTOPHELES. I'll fetch thee fire to dissolve it straight.

    Exit.

FAUSTUS. What might the staying of my blood portend?
    Is it unwilling I should write this bill?   65
    Why streams it not, that I may write afresh?
    'Faustus gives to thee his soul' – ah, there it stayed!
    Why shouldst thou not? Is not thy soul thine own?
    Then write again: 'Faustus gives to thee his soul.'

    Enter MEPHISTOPHELES *with a chafer of coals.*

MEPHISTOPHELES. Here's fire. Come Faustus, set it on.   70

FAUSTUS. So; now the blood begins to clear again,
    Now will I make an end immediately. [*He writes.*]

MEPHISTOPHELES [*aside*]. O, what will not I do to obtain his
    soul?

FAUSTUS. *Consummatum est.* This bill is ended,
    And Faustus hath bequeathed his soul to Lucifer.   75
    But what is this inscription on mine arm?
    '*Homo, fuge!*' Whither should I fly?
    If unto God, he'll throw thee down to hell. –
    My senses are deceived; here's nothing writ. –
    I see it plain. Here in this place is writ   80
    '*Homo, fuge!*' Yet shall not Faustus fly.

MEPHISTOPHELES [*aside*].
    I'll fetch him somewhat to delight his mind.

    Exit. Enter [MEPHISTOPHELES] *with* DEVILS, *giving crowns
    and rich apparel to* FAUSTUS, *and dance and then depart.*

FAUSTUS. Speak, Mephistopheles. What means this show?

MEPHISTOPHELES. Nothing, Faustus, but to delight thy mind
    withal
And to show thee what magic can perform.   85

FAUSTUS. But may I raise up spirits when I please?

MEPHISTOPHELES. Ay, Faustus, and do greater things than these.

FAUSTUS. Then there's enough for a thousand souls.
    Here, Mephistopheles, receive this scroll,
    A deed of gift of body and of soul –   90
    But yet conditionally that thou perform
    All articles prescribed between us both.

MEPHISTOPHELES. Faustus, I swear by hell and Lucifer
    To effect all promises between us made.

FAUSTUS. Then hear me read them.   95

    'On these conditions following:

    First, that Faustus may be a spirit in form and substance.

    Secondly, that Mephistopheles shall be his servant, and at
    his command.

    Thirdly, that Mephistopheles shall do for him and bring   100
    him whatsoever.

    Fourthly, that he shall be in his chamber or house
    invisible.

    Lastly, that he shall appear to the said John Faustus at all
    times in what form or shape soever he please.   105

    I, John Faustus of Wittenberg, Doctor, by these presents,
    do give both body and soul to Lucifer, Prince of the East,
    and his minister Mephistopheles; and furthermore grant
    unto them that four-and-twenty years being expired, the
    articles above written inviolate, full power to fetch or   110
    carry the said John Faustus, body and soul, flesh, blood,
    or goods, into their habitation wheresoever.

                              By me, John Faustus.'

MEPHISTOPHELES. Speak, Faustus. Do you deliver this as
    your deed?   115

FAUSTUS [*giving the deed*]. Ay. Take it, and the devil give thee
    good on't.

MEPHISTOPHELES. Now, Faustus, ask what thou wilt.

FAUSTUS. First will I question with thee about hell.
    Tell me, where is the place that men call hell?   120

MEPHISTOPHELES. Under the heavens.

FAUSTUS.   Ay, but whereabout?

MEPHISTOPHELES. Within the bowels of these elements,
    Where we are tortured and remain for ever.
    Hell hath no limits, nor is circumscribed
    In one self place, for where we are is hell,   125
    And where hell is must we ever be.
    And, to conclude, when all the world dissolves,
    And every creature shall be purified,
    All places shall be hell that is not heaven.

FAUSTUS. Come, I think hell's a fable.   130

MEPHISTOPHELES. Ay, think so still, till experience change
    thy mind.

FAUSTUS. Why, think'st thou then that Faustus shall be damned?

MEPHISTOPHELES. Ay, of necessity, for here's the scroll
    Wherein thou hast given thy soul to Lucifer.

FAUSTUS. Ay, and body too. But what of that?   135
    Think'st thou that Faustus is so fond
    To imagine that after this life there is any pain?
    Tush, these are trifles and mere old wives' tales.

MEPHISTOPHELES. But, Faustus, I am an instance to prove
    the contrary,
    For I am damned and am now in hell.   140

FAUSTUS. How? Now in hell? Nay, an this be hell, I'll
    willingly be damned here. What? Walking, disputing,
    etc.? But leaving off this, let me have a wife, the fairest

maid in Germany, for I am wanton and lascivious and
cannot live without a wife.   145

MEPHISTOPHELES. How, a wife? I prithee, Faustus, talk not
of a wife.

FAUSTUS. Nay, sweet Mephistopheles, fetch me one, for I will
have one.

MEPHISTOPHELES. Well, thou wilt have one. Sit there till
I come.   150
I'll fetch thee a wife, in the devil's name. [*Exit.*]

Enter [MEPHISTOPHELES] *with a* DEVIL *dressed like a woman,
with fireworks.*

MEPHISTOPHELES. Tell, Faustus, how dost thou like thy wife?

FAUSTUS. A plague on her for a hot whore!

MEPHISTOPHELES. Tut, Faustus, marriage is but a ceremonial
toy. If thou lovest me, think no more of it.   155

[*Exit* DEVIL.]

I'll cull thee out the fairest courtesans
And bring them ev'ry morning to thy bed.
She whom thine eye shall like, thy heart shall have,
Be she as chaste as was Penelope,
As wise as Saba, or as beautiful   160
As was bright Lucifer before his fall.

[*Presenting a book.*]

Hold, take this book. Peruse it thoroughly.
The iterating of these lines brings gold;
The framing of this circle on the ground
Brings whirlwinds, tempests, thunder, and lightning.   165
Pronounce this thrice devoutly to thyself,
And men in armour shall appear to thee,
Ready to execute what thou desir'st.

FAUSTUS. Thanks, Mephistopheles. Yet fain would I have a
book wherein I might behold all spells and incantations,   170
that I might raise up spirits when I please.

MEPHISTOPHELES. Here they are in this book.

There turn to them.

FAUSTUS. Now would I have a book where I might see all
    characters and planets of the heavens, that I might know
    their motions and dispositions.   175

MEPHISTOPHELES. Here they are too.

Turn to them.

FAUSTUS. Nay, let me have one book more – and then I have
    done – wherein I might see all plants, herbs, and trees that
    grow upon the earth.

MEPHISTOPHELES. Here they be.   180

Turn to them.

FAUSTUS. O, thou art deceived.

MEPHISTOPHELES. Tut, I warrant thee.

    [*Exeunt.*]

[II.ii]

Enter ROBIN *the ostler with a book in his hand.*

ROBIN. O, this is admirable! Here I ha' stol'n one of Doctor
    Faustus' conjuring books, and, i' faith, I mean to search
    some circles for my own use. Now will I make all the
    maidens in our parish dance at my pleasure stark naked
    before me, and so by that means I shall see more than e'er   5
    I felt or saw yet.

    Enter RAFE, *calling* ROBIN.

RAFE. Robin, prithee, come away. There's a gentleman tarries
    to have his horse, and he would have his things rubbed
    and made clean; he keeps such a chafing with my mistress
    about it, and she has sent me to look thee out. Prithee,   10
    come away.

ROBIN. Keep out, keep out, or else you are blown up, you are
dismembered, Rafe! Keep out, for I am about a roaring piece
of work.

RAFE. Come, what dost thou with that same book? Thou canst   15
not read.

ROBIN. Yes, my master and mistress shall find that I can
read – he for his forehead, she for her private study.
She's born to bear with me, or else my art fails.

RAFE. Why, Robin, what book is that?   20

ROBIN. What book? Why the most intolerable book for conjuring that e'er was invented by any brimstone devil.

RAFE. Canst thou conjure with it?

ROBIN. I can do all these things easily with it: first, I can make
thee drunk with hippocras at any tavern in Europe for   25
nothing. That's one of my conjuring works.

RAFE. Our Master Parson says that's nothing.

ROBIN. True, Rafe; and more, Rafe, if thou hast any mind
to Nan Spit, our kitchen maid, then turn her and wind her
to thy own use as often as thou wilt, and at midnight.   30

RAFE. O brave, Robin! Shall I have Nan Spit, and to mine own
use? On that condition I'll feed thy devil with horse-bread
as long as he lives, of free cost.

ROBIN. No more, sweet Rafe. Let's go and make clean our
boots, which lie foul upon our hands, and then to our   35
conjuring, in the devil's name.

Exeunt.

[II.iii]

[*Enter* FAUSTUS *in his study, and* MEPHISTOPHELES.]

FAUSTUS. When I behold the heavens, then I repent
And curse thee, wicked Mephistopheles,
Because thou hast deprived me of those joys.

MEPHISTOPHELES. Why Faustus,
    Think'st thou heaven is such a glorious thing?   5
    I tell thee, 'tis not half so fair as thou
    Or any man that breathes on earth.

FAUSTUS. How provest thou that?

MEPHISTOPHELES. It was made for man; therefore is man
    more excellent.

FAUSTUS. If it were made for man, 'twas made for me.   10
    I will renounce this magic and repent.

    Enter GOOD ANGEL *and* EVIL ANGEL.

GOOD ANGEL. Faustus, repent yet, God will pity thee.

EVIL ANGEL. Thou art a spirit. God cannot pity thee.

FAUSTUS. Who buzzeth in mine ears I am a spirit?
    Be I a devil, yet God may pity me;   15
    Ay, God will pity me if I repent.

EVIL ANGEL. Ay, but Faustus never shall repent.

    Exeunt [ANGELS].

FAUSTUS. My heart's so hardened I cannot repent.
    Scarce can I name salvation, faith, or heaven
    But fearful echoes thunder in mine ears: 20
    'Faustus, thou art damned!' Then swords and knives,
    Poison, guns, halters, and envenomed steel
    Are laid before me to dispatch myself;
    And long ere this I should have slain myself
    Had not sweet pleasure conquered deep despair.   25
    Have not I made blind Homer sing to me
    Of Alexander's love and Oenone's death?
    And hath not he that built the walls of Thebes
    With ravishing sound of his melodious harp
    Made music with my Mephistopheles?   30
    Why should I die, then, or basely despair?
    I am resolved Faustus shall ne'er repent.
    Come, Mephistopheles, let us dispute again
    And argue of divine astrology.
    Tell me, are there many heavens above the moon?   35

Are all celestial bodies but one globe,
As is the substance of this centric earth?

MEPHISTOPHELES. As are the elements, such are the spheres,
    Mutually folded in each others' orb;
    And, Faustus, all jointly move upon one axletree,   40
    Whose terminine is termed the world's wide pole.
    Nor are the names of Saturn, Mars, or Jupiter
    Feigned, but are erring stars.   44

FAUSTUS. But tell me, have they all one motion, both *situ et tempore*?

MEPHISTOPHELES. All jointly move from east to west in
    four-and-twenty hours upon the poles of the world, but
    differ in their motion upon the poles of the zodiac.

FAUSTUS. Tush, these slender trifles Wagner can decide.
    Hath Mephistopheles no greater skill?   50
    Who knows not the double motion of the planets?
    The first is finished in a natural day,
    The second thus, as Saturn in thirty years,
    Jupiter in twelve, Mars in four, the sun, Venus, and
    Mercury in a year, the moon in twenty-eight days. Tush,   55
    these are freshmen's suppositions. But tell me, hath every
    sphere a dominion or *intelligentia*?

MEPHISTOPHELES. Ay.

FAUSTUS. How many heavens or spheres are there?

MEPHISTOPHELES. Nine: the seven planets, the firmament,   60
    and the empyreal heaven.

FAUSTUS. Well, resolve me in this question: why have we
    not conjunctions, oppositions, aspects, eclipses all at one
    time, but in some years we have more, in some less?

MEPHISTOPHELES. *Per inaequalem motum respectu totius*.   65

FAUSTUS. Well, I am answered. Tell me who made the world.

MEPHISTOPHELES. I will not.

FAUSTUS. Sweet Mephistopheles, tell me.

MEPHISTOPHELES. Move me not, for I will not tell thee.

FAUSTUS. Villain, have I not bound thee to tell me anything?   70

MEPHISTOPHELES. Ay, that is not against our kingdom, but
    this is. Think thou on hell, Faustus, for thou art damned.

FAUSTUS. Think, Faustus, upon God, that made the world.

MEPHISTOPHELES. Remember this.

   Exit.

FAUSTUS. Ay, go, accursèd spirit, to ugly hell!   75
   'Tis thou hast damned distressèd Faustus' soul.
   Is 't not too late?

   Enter GOOD ANGEL *and* EVIL [ANGEL].

EVIL ANGEL. Too late.

GOOD ANGEL. Never too late, if Faustus can repent.

EVIL ANGEL. If thou repent, devils shall tear thee in pieces.   80

GOOD ANGEL. Repent, and they shall never raze thy skin.

   Exeunt [ANGELS].

FAUSTUS. Ah, Christ, my Saviour,
   Seek to save distressèd Faustus' soul!

   Enter LUCIFER, BEELZEBUB, *and* MEPHISTOPHELES.

LUCIFER. Christ cannot save thy soul, for he is just.
   There's none but I have int'rest in the same.   85

FAUSTUS. O, who art thou that look'st so terrible?

LUCIFER. I am Lucifer,
   And this is my companion prince in hell.

FAUSTUS. O Faustus, they are come to fetch away thy soul!

LUCIFER. We come to tell thee thou dost injure us.   90
   Thou talk'st of Christ, contrary to thy promise.
   Thou shouldst not think of God. Think of the devil,
   And of his dame, too.

FAUSTUS. Nor will I henceforth. Pardon me in this,
   And Faustus vows never to look to heaven,   95
   Never to name God or to pray to him,

To burn his Scriptures, slay his ministers,
And make my spirits pull his churches down.

LUCIFER. Do so, and we will highly gratify thee.
Faustus, we are come from hell to show thee some pas-   100
time. Sit down, and thou shalt see all the Seven Deadly
Sins appear in their proper shapes.

FAUSTUS. That sight will be as pleasing unto me as paradise
was to Adam the first day of his creation.   104

LUCIFER. Talk not of paradise nor creation, but mark this show.
Talk of the devil, and nothing else. –
[*Calling offstage.*] Come away!

[FAUSTUS *sits.*] *Enter the* SEVEN DEADLY SINS.

Now, Faustus, examine them of their several names and
dispositions.

FAUSTUS. What art thou, the first?   110

PRIDE. I am Pride. I disdain to have any parents. I am like
to Ovid's flea: I can creep into every corner of a wench.
Sometimes like a periwig I sit upon her brow, or like a
fan of feathers I kiss her lips. Indeed I do – what do I
not? But fie, what a scent is here! I'll not speak another   115
word, except the ground were perfumed and covered with
cloth of arras.

FAUSTUS. What art thou, the second?

COVETOUSNESS. I am Covetousness, begotten of an old
churl in an old leathern bag; and might I have my wish,   120
I would desire that this house and all the people in it were
turned to gold, that I might lock you up in my good chest.
O my sweet gold!

FAUSTUS. What art thou, the third?

WRATH. I am Wrath. I had neither father nor mother.   125
I leaped out of a lion's mouth when I was scarce half an
hour old, and ever since I have run up and down the world
with this case of rapiers, wounding myself when I had nobody
to fight withal. I was born in hell, and look to it, for some
of you shall be my father.   130

FAUSTUS. What art thou, the fourth?

ENVY. I am Envy, begotten of a chimney-sweeper and an
oyster-wife. I cannot read, and therefore wish all books
were burnt. I am lean with seeing others eat. O, that
there would come a famine through all the world, that all   135
might die, and I live alone! Then thou shouldst see how
fat I would be. But must thou sit and I stand? Come
down, with a vengeance!

FAUSTUS. Away, envious rascal! – What are thou, the fifth?

GLUTTONY. Who, I, sir? I am Gluttony. My parents are all   140
dead, and the devil a penny they have left me but a bare
pension, and that is thirty meals a day, and ten bevers –
a small trifle to suffice nature. O, I come of a royal parent-
age. My grandfather was a gammon of bacon, my grand-
mother a hogshead of claret wine. My godfathers were   145
these: Peter Pickle-herring and Martin Martlemas-beef.
O, but my godmother, she was a jolly gentlewoman, and
well beloved in every good town and city; her name was
Mistress Margery March-beer. Now, Faustus, thou hast
heard all my progeny, wilt thou bid me to supper?   150

FAUSTUS. No, I'll see thee hanged. Thou wilt eat up all my
victuals.

GLUTTONY. Then the devil choke thee!

FAUSTUS. Choke thyself, glutton! – What art thou, the sixth?

SLOTH. I am Sloth. I was begotten on a sunny bank, where   155
I have lain ever since, and you have done me great injury
to bring me from thence. Let me be carried thither again
by Gluttony and Lechery. I'll not speak another word for
a king's ransom.

FAUSTUS. What are you, Mistress Minx, the seventh and last?   160

LECHERY. Who, I, sir? I am one that loves an inch of raw
mutton better than an ell of fried stockfish, and the first
letter of my name begins with lechery.

LUCIFER. Away, to hell, to hell!

Exeunt the SINS.

Now, Faustus, how dost thou like this?   165

FAUSTUS. O, this feeds my soul!

LUCIFER. Tut, Faustus, in hell is all manner of delight.

FAUSTUS. O, might I see hell and return again, how happy
    were I then!

LUCIFER. Thou shalt. I will send for thee at midnight.   170
    [*Presenting a book.*] In meantime, take this book. Peruse
    it throughly, and thou shalt turn thyself into what shape
    thou wilt.

FAUSTUS [*taking the book*]. Great thanks, mighty Lucifer.
    This will I keep as chary as my life.   175

LUCIFER. Farewell, Faustus, and think on the devil.

FAUSTUS. Farewell, great Lucifer. Come, Mephistopheles.

    Exeunt omnes, [different ways].

Act III

[III.Chorus]

Enter WAGNER *solus.*

WAGNER. Learnèd Faustus,
    To know the secrets of astronomy
    Graven in the book of Jove's high firmament,
    Did mount himself to scale Olympus' top,
    Being seated in a chariot burning bright   5
    Drawn by the strength of yoky dragons' necks.
    He now is gone to prove cosmography,
    And, as I guess, will first arrive at Rome
    To see the Pope and manner of his court
    And take some part of holy Peter's feast   10
    That to this day is highly solemnised.

    Exit WAGNER.

[III.i]

Enter FAUSTUS *and* MEPHISTOPHELES.

FAUSTUS. Having now, my good Mephistopheles,
    Passed with delight the stately town of Trier,
    Environed round with airy mountain-tops,
    With walls of flint and deep intrenchèd lakes,
    Not to be won by any conquering prince;   5
    From Paris next, coasting the realm of France,
    We saw the river Maine fall into Rhine,
    Whose banks are set with groves of fruitful vines.
    Then up to Naples, rich Campania,
    Whose buildings, fair and gorgeous to the eye,   10

The streets straight forth and paved with finest brick,
Quarters the town in four equivalents.
There saw we learnèd Maro's golden tomb,
The way he cut an English mile in length
Thorough a rock of stone in one night's space.   15
From thence to Venice, Padua, and the rest,
In midst of which a sumptuous temple stands
That threats the stars with her aspiring top.
Thus hitherto hath Faustus spent his time.
But tell me now, what resting place is this?   20
Hast thou, as erst I did command,
Conducted me within the walls of Rome?

MEPHISTOPHELES. Faustus, I have. And because we will
    not be unprovided, I have taken up his Holiness' privy
    chamber for our use.   25

FAUSTUS. I hope his Holiness will bid us welcome.

MEPHISTOPHELES. Tut, 'tis no matter, man. We'll be
    bold with his good cheer.
And now, my Faustus, that thou mayst perceive
What Rome containeth to delight thee with,   30
Know that this city stands upon seven hills
That underprops the groundwork of the same.
Just through the midst runs flowing Tiber's stream,
With winding banks that cut it in two parts,
Over the which four stately bridges lean,   35
That makes safe passage to each part of Rome.
Upon the bridge called Ponte Angelo
Erected is a castle passing strong,
Within whose walls such store of ordnance are,
And double cannons, framed of carvèd brass,   40
As match the days within one complete year –
Besides the gates and high pyramides
Which Julius Caesar brought from Africa.

FAUSTUS. Now, by the kingdoms of infernal rule,
Of Styx, Acheron, and the fiery lake   45
Of ever-burning Phlegethon, I swear
That I do long to see the monuments

And situation of bright splendent Rome.
Come, therefore, let's away!

MEPHISTOPHELES. Nay, Faustus, stay. I know you'd fain
    see the Pope   50
And take some part of holy Peter's feast,
Where thou shalt see a troupe of bald-pate friars
Whose *summum bonum* is in belly cheer.

FAUSTUS. Well, I am content to compass then some sport,
    And by their folly make us merriment.   55
Then charm me that I may be invisible, to do what
I please unseen of any whilst I stay in Rome.

MEPHISTOPHELES [*placing a robe on* FAUSTUS]. So, Faustus, now
    do what thou wilt, thou shalt not be discerned.

Sound a sennet. Enter the POPE *and the* CARDINAL OF
LORRAINE *to the banquet, with* FRIARS *attending.*

POPE. My lord of Lorraine, will 't please you draw near?   60

FAUSTUS. Fall to, and the devil choke you an you spare.

POPE. How now, who's that which spake? Friars, look about.

FRIAR. Here's nobody, if it like your Holiness.

POPE. My lord, here is a dainty dish was sent me from the
    Bishop of Milan.

    [*He presents a dish.*]   65

FAUSTUS. I thank you, sir.

    Snatch it.

POPE. How now, who's that which snatched the meat from
    me? Will no man look? – My lord, this dish was sent me
    from the Cardinal of Florence.

FAUSTUS [*snatching the dish*]. You say true. I'll ha 't.   70

POPE. What again? – My lord, I'll drink to your Grace.

FAUSTUS [*snatching the cup*]. I'll pledge your Grace.

LORRAINE. My lord, it may be some ghost, newly crept out
    of purgatory, come to beg a pardon of your Holiness.

POPE. It may be so. Friars, prepare a dirge to lay the fury of   75
    this ghost. Once again, my lord, fall to.

    The POPE *crosseth himself.*

FAUSTUS. What, are you crossing of yourself? Well, use that
    trick no more, I would advise you.

    [*The* POPE] *cross[es himself] again.*

    Well, there's a second time. Aware the third, I give you
    fair warning.   80

    [*The* POPE] *cross[es himself] again, and* FAUSTUS *hits him a
    box of the ear, and they all run away.*

    Come on, Mephistopheles. What shall we do?

MEPHISTOPHELES. Nay, I know not. We shall be cursed with
    bell, book, and candle.

FAUSTUS. How? Bell, book, and candle, candle, book, and bell,
    Forward and backward, to curse Faustus to hell.   85
    Anon you shall hear a hog grunt, a calf bleat, and an ass bray,
    Because it is Saint Peter's holy day.

    Enter all the FRIARS *to sing the dirge.*

FRIAR. Come, brethren, let's about our business with good
    devotion.   89

    [*The* FRIARS] *sing this:*

    Cursèd be he that stole away his Holiness' meat from the table.
        Maledicat Dominus!
    Cursèd be he that struck his Holiness a blow on the face.
        Maledicat Dominus!
    Cursèd be he that took Friar Sandelo a blow on the pate.
        Maledicat Dominus!   95
    Cursèd be he that disturbeth our holy dirge.
        Maledicat Dominus!
    Cursèd be he that took away his Holiness' wine.
        Maledicat Dominus!
    Et omnes sancti. Amen.   100

    [FAUSTUS *and* MEPHISTOPHELES] *beat the* FRIARS, *and fling
fireworks among them, and so exeunt.*

[III.ii]

Enter ROBIN [*with a conjuring book*] *and* RAFE *with a silver goblet.*

ROBIN. Come, Rafe, did not I tell thee we were for ever made
by this Doctor Faustus' book? *Ecce signum!* Here's a simple
purchase for horse-keepers. Our horses shall eat no hay as
long as this lasts.

Enter the VINTNER.

RAFE. But Robin, here comes the Vintner.   5

ROBIN. Hush, I'll gull him supernaturally. – Drawer, I hope
all is paid. God be with you. Come, Rafe.

[*They start to go.*]

VINTNER [*to* ROBIN]. Soft, sir, a word with you. I must yet
have a goblet paid from you ere you go.

ROBIN. I, a goblet? Rafe, I, a goblet? I scorn you, and you are   10
but a etc. I, a goblet? Search me.

VINTNER. I mean so, sir, with your favour.

[*The* VINTNER *searches* ROBIN.]

ROBIN. How say you now?

VINTNER. I must say somewhat to your fellow – you, sir.

RAFE. Me, sir? Me, sir? Search your fill.   15

[*He gives the goblet to* ROBIN; *then the* VINTNER *searches* RAFE.]

Now, sir, you may be ashamed to burden honest men with a
matter of truth.

VINTNER. Well, t'one of you hath this goblet about you.

ROBIN. You lie, drawer, 'tis afore me. Sirrah, you, I'll teach
ye to impeach honest men. Stand by. I'll scour you for a   20
goblet. Stand aside, you had best, I charge you in the name
of Beelzebub. [*Tossing the goblet to* RAFE.] Look to the goblet,
Rafe.

VINTNER. What mean you, sirrah?

ROBIN. I'll tell you what I mean.   25

He reads.

Sanctobulorum Periphrasticon! Nay, I'll tickle you, Vintner. Look
to the goblet, Rafe. *Polypragmos Belseborams framanto pacostiphos
tostu Mephistopheles!* etc.

Enter to them MEPHISTOPHELES.

[*Exit the* VINTNER, *running.*]

MEPHISTOPHELES. Monarch of hell, under whose black survey
Great potentates do kneel with awful fear,   30
Upon whose altars thousand souls do lie,
How am I vexèd with these villains' charms!
From Constantinople am I hither come
Only for pleasure of these damnèd slaves.

ROBIN. How, from Constantinople? You have had a great   35
journey. Will you take sixpence in your purse to pay for your
supper and be gone?

MEPHISTOPHELES. Well, villains, for your presumption I
transform thee [*To* ROBIN.] into an ape and thee [*To* RAFE.]
into a dog. And so, begone!   40

Exit.

ROBIN. How, into an ape? That's brave. I'll have fine sport
with the boys; I'll get nuts and apples enough.

RAFE. And I must be a dog.

ROBIN. I' faith, thy head will never be out of the pottage pot.

Exeunt.

Act IV

[IV.Chorus]

Enter CHORUS.

CHORUS. When Faustus had with pleasure ta'en the view
    Of rarest things and royal courts of kings,
    He stayed his course and so returnèd home,
    Where such as bear his absence but with grief –
    I mean his friends and nearest companions –   5
    Did gratulate his safety with kind words.
    And in their conference of what befell,
    Touching his journey through the world and air,
    They put forth questions of astrology,
    Which Faustus answered with such learnèd skill   10
    As they admired and wondered at his wit.
    Now is his fame spread forth in every land.
    Amongst the rest the Emperor is one,
    Carolus the Fifth, at whose palace now
    Faustus is feasted 'mongst his noblemen.   15
    What there he did in trial of his art
    I leave untold, your eyes shall see performed.

    Exit.

[IV.i]

Enter EMPEROR, FAUSTUS, [MEPHISTOPHELES,] *and a*
KNIGHT, *with* ATTENDANTS.

EMPEROR. Master Doctor Faustus, I have heard strange
    report of thy knowledge in the black art – how that none in
    my empire, nor in the whole world, can compare with thee

for the rare effects of magic. They say thou hast a familiar
spirit by whom thou canst accomplish what thou list.   5
This, therefore, is my request: that thou let me see some
proof of thy skill, that mine eyes may be witnesses to
confirm what mine ears have heard reported. And here
I swear to thee, by the honour of mine imperial crown,
that whatever thou dost, thou shalt be no ways prejudiced   10
or endamaged.

KNIGHT (*aside*). I' faith, he looks much like a conjurer.

FAUSTUS. My gracious sovereign, though I must confess
    myself far inferior to the report men have published, and
    nothing answerable to the honour of your Imperial   15
    Majesty, yet, for that love and duty binds me thereunto,
    I am content to do whatsoever your Majesty shall com-
    mand me.

EMPEROR. Then, Doctor Faustus, mark what I shall say.
    As I was sometime solitary set   20
    Within my closet, sundry thoughts arose
    About the honour of mine ancestors –
    How they had won by prowess such exploits,
    Got such riches, subdued so many kingdoms
    As we that do succeed or they that shall   25
    Hereafter possess our throne shall,
    I fear me, never attain to that degree
    Of high renown and great authority.
    Amongst which kings is Alexander the Great,
    Chief spectacle of the world's pre-eminence,   30
    The bright shining of whose glorious acts
    Lightens the world with his reflecting beams –
    As when I hear but motion made of him,
    It grieves my soul I never saw the man.
    If, therefore, thou by cunning of thine art   35
    Canst raise this man from hollow vaults below
    Where lies entombed this famous conqueror,
    And bring with him his beauteous paramour,
    Both in their right shapes, gesture, and attire
    They used to wear during their time of life,   40

Thou shalt both satisfy my just desire
And give me cause to praise thee whilst I live.

FAUSTUS. My gracious lord, I am ready to accomplish your
request, so far forth as by art and power of my spirit I am
able to perform.   45

KNIGHT (*aside*). I'faith, that's just nothing at all.

FAUSTUS. But if it like your Grace, it is not in my ability
to present before your eyes the true substantial bodies of
those two deceased princes, which long since are con-
sumed to dust.   50

KNIGHT (*aside*). Ay, marry, Master Doctor, now there's a
sign of grace in you, when you will confess the truth.

FAUSTUS. But such spirits as can lively resemble Alexander
and his paramour shall appear before your Grace in that
manner that they best lived in, in their most flourishing   55
estate – which I doubt not shall sufficiently content your
Imperial Majesty.

EMPEROR. Go to, Master Doctor. Let me see them presently.

KNIGHT. Do you hear, Master Doctor? You bring Alexander
and his paramour before the Emperor?   60

FAUSTUS. How then, sir?

KNIGHT. I' faith, that's as true as Diana turned me to a stag.

FAUSTUS. No, sir, but when Actaeon died, he left the horns for
you. [*Aside to* MEPHISTOPHELES.] Mephistopheles, begone!

Exit MEPHISTOPHELES.

KNIGHT. Nay, an you go to conjuring, I'll be gone.   65

Exit KNIGHT.

FAUSTUS (*aside*). I'll meet with you anon for interrupting me
so. – Here they are, my gracious lord.

Enter MEPHISTOPHELES *with* ALEXANDER *and his*
PARAMOUR.

EMPEROR. Master Doctor, I heard this lady while she lived
    had a wart or mole in her neck. How shall I know whether it
    be so or no?   70

FAUSTUS. Your Highness may boldly go and see.

[*The* EMPEROR *makes an inspection, and then*] *exeunt*
ALEXANDER [*and his* PARAMOUR].

EMPEROR. Sure these are no spirits, but the true substantial
    bodies of those two deceased princes.

FAUSTUS. Will't please your Highness now to send for the
    knight that was so pleasant with me here of late?   75

EMPEROR. One of you call him forth.

[*An* ATTENDANT *goes to summon the* KNIGHT.] *Enter the*
KNIGHT *with a pair of horns on his head.*

How now, sir knight? Why, I had thought thou hadst
    been a bachelor, but now I see thou hast a wife, that not
    only gives thee horns but makes thee wear them. Feel on
    thy head.   80

KNIGHT [*to* FAUSTUS]. Thou damnèd wretch and execrable dog,
    Bred in the concave of some monstrous rock,
    How dar'st thou thus abuse a gentleman?
    Villain, I say, undo what thou hast done.

FAUSTUS. O, not so fast, sir. There's no haste but good.   85
    Are you remembered how you crossed me in my conference
    with the Emperor? I think I have met with you for it.

EMPEROR. Good Master Doctor, at my entreaty release him.
    He hath done penance sufficient.

FAUSTUS. My gracious lord, not so much for the injury he   90
    offered me here in your presence as to delight you with
    some mirth hath Faustus worthily requited this injurious
    knight; which being all I desire, I am content to release
    him of his horns. – And, sir knight, hereafter speak well
    of scholars. [*Aside to* MEPHISTOPHELES.] Mephistopheles,   95
    transform him straight. [*The horns are removed.*] Now, my
    good lord, having done my duty, I humbly take my leave.

EMPEROR. Farewell, Master Doctor. Yet, ere you go,
    Expect from me a bounteous reward.

    Exeunt EMPEROR, [KNIGHT, *and* ATTENDANTS].

FAUSTUS. Now, Mephistopheles, the restless course   100
    That time doth run with calm and silent foot,
    Short'ning my days and thread of vital life,
    Calls for the payment of my latest years.
    Therefore, sweet Mephistopheles, let us make haste
    To Wittenberg.   105

MEPHISTOPHELES. What, will you go on horseback or on foot?

FAUSTUS. Nay, till I am past this fair and pleasant green,
    I'll walk on foot.

    Enter a HORSE-COURSER.

HORSE-COURSER. I have been all this day seeking one
    Master Fustian. Mass, see where he is. – God save you,   110
    Master Doctor.

FAUSTUS. What, Horse-courser! You are well met.

HORSE-COURSER [*offering money*]. Do you hear, sir? I have
    brought you forty dollars for your horse.

FAUSTUS. I cannot sell him so. If thou lik'st him for fifty,   115
    take him.

HORSE-COURSER. Alas, sir, I have no more.
    [*To* MEPHISTOPHELES.] I pray you, speak for me.

MEPHISTOPHELES [*to* FAUSTUS]. I pray you, let him
    have him. He is an honest fellow, and he has a great   120
    charge, neither wife nor child.

FAUSTUS. Well, come, give me your money. [*He takes the
    money.*] My boy will deliver him to you. But I must tell
    you one thing before you have him: ride him not into the
    water, at any hand.   125

HORSE-COURSER. Why, sir, will he not drink of all waters?

FAUSTUS. O, yes, he will drink of all waters, but ride him not

into the water. Ride him over hedge, or ditch, or where
thou wilt, but not into the water.

HORSE-COURSER. Well, sir [*Aside.*] Now am I made man   130
for ever. I'll not leave my horse for forty. If he had but
the quality of hey, ding, ding, hey, ding, ding, I'd make
a brave living on him; he has a buttock as slick as an eel.
[*To* FAUSTUS.] Well, goodbye, sir. Your boy will deliver
him me? But hark ye, sir: if my horse be sick or ill at ease,   135
if I bring his water to you, you'll tell me what it is?

FAUSTUS. Away, you villain! What, dost think I am a horse
doctor?

Exit HORSE-COURSER.

What art thou, Faustus, but a man condemned to die?
Thy fatal time doth draw to final end.   140
Despair doth drive distrust unto my thoughts.
Confound these passions with a quiet sleep.
Tush! Christ did call the thief upon the cross;
Then rest thee, Faustus, quiet in conceit.

Sleep in his chair.

Enter HORSE-COURSER *all wet, crying.*

HORSE-COURSER. Alas, alas! 'Doctor' Fustian, quotha!   145
Mass, Doctor Lopus was never such a doctor. H'as given me
a purgation, h'as purged me of forty dollars. I shall never
see them more. But yet, like an ass as I was, I would not
be ruled by him, for he bade me I should ride him into
no water. Now I, thinking my horse had had some rare   150
quality that he would not have had me known of, I, like
a venturous youth, rid him into the deep pond at the
town's end. I was no sooner in the middle of the pond but
my horse vanished away and I sat upon a bottle of hay,
never so near drowning in my life. But I'll seek out my   155
doctor and have my forty dollars again, or I'll make it the
dearest horse! O, yonder is his snipper-snapper. – Do you
hear? You, hey-pass, where's your master?

MEPHISTOPHELES. Why, sir, what would you? You cannot
speak with him.   160

HORSE-COURSER. But I will speak with him.

MEPHISTOPHELES. Why, he's fast asleep. Come some other time.

HORSE-COURSER. I'll speak with him now, or I'll break his
    glass windows about his ears.   164

MEPHISTOPHELES. I tell thee he has not slept this eight nights.

HORSE-COURSER. An he have not slept this eight weeks, I'll
    speak with him.

MEPHISTOPHELES. See where he is, fast asleep.

HORSE-COURSER. Ay, this is he. – God save ye, Master
    Doctor. Master Doctor, Master Doctor Fustian! Forty   170
    dollars, forty dollars for a bottle of hay!

MEPHISTOPHELES. Why, thou seest he hears thee not.

HORSE-COURSER (*holler in his ear*). So-ho, ho! So-ho, ho!
    No, will you not wake? I'll make you wake ere I go.

Pull him by the leg, and pull it away.

Alas, I am undone! What shall I do?   175

FAUSTUS. O my leg, my leg! Help, Mephistopheles! Call the
    officers! My leg, my leg!

MEPHISTOPHELES [*seizing the* HORSE-COURSER]. Come,
    villain, to the constable.

HORSE-COURSER. O Lord, sir, let me go, and I'll give you   180
    forty dollars more.

MEPHISTOPHELES. Where be they?

HORSE-COURSER. I have none about me. Come to my hostry,
    and I'll give them you.

MEPHISTOPHELES. Begone, quickly.   185

    HORSE-COURSER *runs away.*

FAUSTUS. What, is he gone? Farewell, he! Faustus has his
    leg again, and the Horse-courser, I take it, a bottle of hay
    for his labour. Well, this trick shall cost him forty dollars
    more.

Enter WAGNER.

How now, Wagner, what's the news with thee?   190

WAGNER. Sir, the Duke of Vanholt doth earnestly entreat your
    company.

FAUSTUS. The Duke of Vanholt! An honourable gentleman,
    to whom I must be no niggard of my cunning. Come,
    Mephistopheles, let's away to him.   195

Exeunt.

[IV.ii]

[*Enter* FAUSTUS *with* MEPHISTOPHELES.] *Enter to them
the* DUKE [OF VANHOLT] *and the* [*pregnant*] DUCHESS.
The DUKE *speaks.*

DUKE. Believe me, Master Doctor, this merriment hath much
    pleased me.

FAUSTUS. My gracious lord, I am glad it contents you so
    well. – But it may be, madam, you take no delight in
    this. I have heard that great-bellied women do long for   5
    some dainties or other. What is it, madam? Tell me, and
    you shall have it.

DUCHESS. Thanks, good Master Doctor. And, for I see your
    courteous intent to pleasure me, I will not hide from you
    the thing my heart desires. And were it now summer, as   10
    it is January and the dead time of the winter, I would
    desire no better meat than a dish of ripe grapes.

FAUSTUS. Alas, madam, that's nothing. [*Aside to*
    MEPHISTOPHELES.] Mephistopheles, begone!

Exit MEPHISTOPHELES.

Were it a greater thing than this, so it would content you,   15
you should have it.

Enter MEPHISTOPHELES *with the grapes.*

Here they be, madam. Will 't please you taste on them?

[*The* DUCHESS *tastes the grapes.*]

DUKE. Believe me, Master Doctor, this makes me wonder
    above the rest, that, being in the dead time of winter and
    in the month of January, how you should come by these   20
    grapes.

FAUSTUS. If it like your Grace, the year is divided into two
    circles over the whole world, that when it is here winter
    with us, in the contrary circle it is summer with them, as
    in India, Saba, and farther countries in the East; and by   25
    means of a swift spirit that I have, I had them brought
    hither, as ye see. – How do you like them, madam? Be
    they good?

DUCHESS. Believe me, Master Doctor, they be the best grapes
    that e'er I tasted in my life before.   30

FAUSTUS. I am glad they content you so, madam.

DUKE. Come, madam, let us in,
    Where you must well reward this learnèd man
    For the great kindness he hath showed to you.

DUCHESS. And so I will, my lord, and whilst I live   35
    Rest beholding for this courtesy.

FAUSTUS. I humbly thank your Grace.

DUKE. Come, Master Doctor, follow us and receive your reward.

    Exeunt.

Act V

[V.i]

Enter WAGNER *solus.*

WAGNER. I think my master means to die shortly,
    For he hath given to me all his goods.
    And yet methinks if that death were near
    He would not banquet and carouse and swill
    Amongst the students, as even now he doth,   5
    Who are at supper with such belly-cheer
    As Wagner ne'er beheld in all his life.
    See where they come. Belike the feast is ended.

    [*Exit.*]

Enter FAUSTUS *with two or three* SCHOLARS [*and*
MEPHISTOPHELES].

FIRST SCHOLAR. Master Doctor Faustus, since our confer-
    ence about fair ladies – which was the beautifull'st in all the   10
    world – we have determined with ourselves that Helen of
    Greece was the admirablest lady that ever lived. There-
    fore, Master Doctor, if you will do us that favour as to let
    us see that peerless dame of Greece, whom all the world
    admires for majesty, we should think ourselves much   15
    beholding unto you.

FAUSTUS. Gentlemen,
    For that I know your friendship is unfeigned,
    And Faustus' custom is not to deny
    The just requests of those that wish him well,   20
    You shall behold that peerless dame of Greece
    No otherways for pomp and majesty
    Than when Sir Paris crossed the seas with her
    And brought the spoils to rich Dardania.
    Be silent then, for danger is in words.   25

[MEPHISTOPHELES *goes to the door.*] *Music sounds.* [MEPHIS-
TOPHELES *returns,*] *and* HELEN *passeth over the stage.*

SECOND SCHOLAR. Too simple is my wit to tell her praise,
    Whom all the world admires for majesty.

THIRD SCHOLAR. No marvel though the angry Greeks pursued
    With ten years' war the rape of such a queen,
    Whose heavenly beauty passeth all compare.   30

FIRST SCHOLAR. Since we have seen the pride of nature's works
    And only paragon of excellence,

    Enter an OLD MAN.

    Let us depart; and for this glorious deed
    Happy and blest be Faustus evermore.

FAUSTUS. Gentlemen, farewell. The same I wish to you.   35

    Exeunt SCHOLARS.

OLD MAN. Ah, Doctor Faustus, that I might prevail
    To guide thy steps unto the way of life,
    By which sweet path thou mayst attain the goal
    That shall conduct thee to celestial rest!
    Break heart, drop blood, and mingle it with tears –   40
    Tears falling from repentant heaviness
    Of thy most vile and loathsome filthiness,
    The stench whereof corrupts the inward soul
    With such flagitious crimes of heinous sins
    As no commiseration may expel   45
    But mercy, Faustus, of thy Saviour sweet,
    Whose blood alone must wash away thy guilt.

FAUSTUS. Where art thou, Faustus? Wretch, what hast thou done?
    Damned art thou, Faustus, damned! Despair and die!
    Hell calls for right, and with a roaring voice   50
    Says, 'Faustus, come! Thine hour is come.'

    MEPHISTOPHELES *gives him a dagger.*

    And Faustus will come to do thee right.

    [FAUSTUS *prepares to stab himself.*]

OLD MAN. Ah, stay, good Faustus, stay thy desperate steps!
    I see an angel hovers o'er thy head,
    And with a vial full of precious grace   55
    Offers to pour the same into thy soul.
    Then call for mercy and avoid despair.

FAUSTUS. Ah, my sweet friend, I feel thy words
    To comfort my distressèd soul.
    Leave me a while to ponder on my sins   60

OLD MAN. I go, sweet Faustus, but with heavy cheer,
    Fearing the ruin of thy hopeless soul.

    [*Exit.*]

FAUSTUS. Accursèd Faustus, where is mercy now?
    I do repent, and yet I do despair.
    Hell strives with grace for conquest in my breast.   65
    What shall I do to shun the snares of death?

MEPHISTOPHELES. Thou traitor, Faustus, I arrest thy soul
    For disobedience to my sovereign lord.
    Revolt, or I'll in piecemeal tear thy flesh.

FAUSTUS. Sweet Mephistopheles, entreat thy lord   70
    To pardon my unjust presumption,
    And with my blood again I will confirm
    My former vow I made to Lucifer.

MEPHISTOPHELES. Do it then quickly, with unfeignèd heart,
    Lest greater danger do attend thy drift.   75

    [FAUSTUS *cuts his arm and writes with his blood.*]

FAUSTUS. Torment, sweet friend, that base and crooked age
    That durst dissuade me from thy Lucifer,
    With greatest torments that our hell affords.

MEPHISTOPHELES. His faith is great. I cannot touch his soul.
    But what I may afflict his body with   80
    I will attempt, which is but little worth.

FAUSTUS. One thing, good servant, let me crave of thee
    To glut the longing of my heart's desire:
    That I might have unto my paramour

That heavenly Helen which I saw of late,   85
Whose sweet embracings may extinguish clean
These thoughts that do dissuade me from my vow,
And keep mine oath I made to Lucifer.

MEPHISTOPHELES. Faustus, this, or what else thou shalt desire,
Shall be performed in twinkling of an eye.   90

Enter HELEN [*brought in by* MEPHISTOPHELES].

FAUSTUS. Was this the face that launched a thousand ships
And burnt the topless towers of Ilium?
Sweet Helen, make me immortal with a kiss.

[*They kiss.*]

Her lips sucks forth my soul. See where it flies!
Come, Helen, come, give me my soul again.   95

[*They kiss again.*]

Here will I dwell, for heaven be in these lips,
And all is dross that is not Helena.

Enter OLD MAN.

I will be Paris, and for love of thee
Instead of Troy shall Wittenberg be sacked,
And I will combat with weak Menelaus,   100
And wear thy colours on my plumèd crest.
Yea, I will wound Achilles in the heel
And then return to Helen for a kiss.
O, thou art fairer than the evening air,
Clad in the beauty of a thousand stars.   105
Brighter art thou than flaming Jupiter
When he appeared to hapless Semele,
More lovely than the monarch of the sky
In wanton Arethusa's azured arms;
And none but thou shalt be my paramour.   110

Exeunt [FAUSTUS *and* HELEN].

OLD MAN. Accursèd Faustus, miserable man,
That from thy soul exclud'st the grace of heaven
And fliest the throne of His tribunal seat!

Enter the DEVILS. [*They menace the* OLD MAN.]

Satan begins to sift me with his pride.
As in this furnace God shall try my faith,   115
My faith, vile hell, shall triumph over thee.
Ambitious fiends, see how the heavens smiles
At your repulse and laughs your state to scorn!
Hence, hell! For hence I fly unto my God.

Exeunt [*different ways*].

[V.ii]

Enter FAUSTUS *with the* SCHOLARS.

FAUSTUS. Ah, gentlemen!

FIRST SCHOLAR. What ails Faustus?

FAUSTUS. Ah, my sweet chamber-fellow! Had I lived with
    thee, then had I lived still, but now I die eternally. Look,
    comes he not? Comes he not?   5

SECOND SCHOLAR. What means Faustus?

THIRD SCHOLAR. Belike he is grown into some sickness by
    being over-solitary.

FIRST SCHOLAR. If it be so, we'll have physicians to cure
    him. [*To* FAUSTUS.] 'Tis but a surfeit. Never fear, man.   10

FAUSTUS. A surfeit of deadly sin that hath damned both body
    and soul.

SECOND SCHOLAR. Yet, Faustus, look up to heaven.
    Remember God's mercies are infinite.

FAUSTUS. But Faustus' offence can ne'er be pardoned. The   15
    serpent that tempted Eve may be saved, but not Faustus.
    Ah, gentlemen, hear me with patience, and tremble not
    at my speeches. Though my heart pants and quivers to
    remember that I have been a student here these thirty
    years, O, would I had never seen Wittenberg, never read   20

book! And what wonders I have done, all Germany
can witness, yea, all the world, for which Faustus hath
lost both Germany and the world, yea, heaven itself –
heaven, the seat of God, the throne of the blessed, the
kingdom of joy – and must remain in hell for ever. Hell,   25
ah, hell for ever! Sweet friends, what shall become of
Faustus, being in hell for ever?

THIRD SCHOLAR. Yet, Faustus, call on God.

FAUSTUS. On God, whom Faustus hath abjured? On God,
whom Faustus hath blasphemed? Ah, my God, I would   30
weep, but the devil draws in my tears. Gush forth blood
instead of tears, yea, life and soul. O, he stays my tongue!
I would lift up my hands, but see, they hold them, they
hold them.

ALL. Who, Faustus?   35

FAUSTUS. Lucifer and Mephistopheles. Ah, gentlemen! I gave
them my soul for my cunning.

ALL. God forbid!

FAUSTUS. God forbade it indeed, but Faustus hath done it.
For vain pleasure of four-and-twenty years hath Faustus   40
lost eternal joy and felicity. I writ them a bill with mine
own blood. The date is expired, the time will come, and
he will fetch me.

FIRST SCHOLAR. Why did not Faustus tell us of this before,
that divines might have prayed for thee?   45

FAUSTUS. Oft have I thought to have done so, but the devil
threatened to tear me in pieces if I named God, to fetch
both body and soul if I once gave ear to divinity. And
now 'tis too late. Gentlemen, away, lest you perish
with me.   50

SECOND SCHOLAR. O, what shall we do to save Faustus?

FAUSTUS. Talk not of me, but save yourselves and depart.

THIRD SCHOLAR. God will strengthen me. I will stay with
Faustus.

FIRST SCHOLAR [*to the* THIRD SCHOLAR]. Tempt not   55
    God, sweet friend, but let us into the next room and there
    pray for him.

FAUSTUS. Ay, pray for me, pray for me! And what noise soever
    ye hear, come not unto me, for nothing can rescue me.

SECOND SCHOLAR. Pray thou, and we will pray that God   60
    may have mercy upon thee.

FAUSTUS. Gentlemen, farewell. If I live till morning, I'll visit
    you; if not, Faustus is gone to hell.

ALL. Faustus, farewell.

    Exeunt SCHOLARS.

    The clock strikes eleven.

FAUSTUS. Ah, Faustus,   65
    Now hast thou but one bare hour to live,
    And then thou must be damned perpetually.
    Stand still, you ever-moving spheres of heaven,
    That time may cease and midnight never come!
    Fair nature's eye, rise, rise again, and make   70
    Perpetual day; or let this hour be but
    A year, a month, a week, a natural day,
    That Faustus may repent and save his soul!
    O lente, lente currite noctis equi!
    The stars move still; time runs; the clock will strike;   75
    The devil will come, and Faustus must be damned.
    O, I'll leap up to my God! Who pulls me down?
    See, see where Christ's blood streams in the firmament!
    One drop would save my soul, half a drop. Ah, my Christ!
    Ah, rend not my heart for naming of my Christ!   80
    Yet will I call on him. O, spare me, Lucifer!
    Where is it now? 'Tis gone; and see where God
    Stretcheth out his arm and bends his ireful brows!
    Mountains and hills, come, come and fall on me,
    And hide me from the heavy wrath of God!   85
    No, no!
    Then will I headlong run into the earth.
    Earth, gape! O, no, it will not harbour me.

You stars that reigned at my nativity,
Whose influence hath allotted death and hell,   90
Now draw up Faustus like a foggy mist
Into the entrails of yon labouring cloud,
That when you vomit forth into the air,
My limbs may issue from your smoky mouths,
So that my soul may but ascend to heaven.   95

The watch strikes.

Ah, half the hour is past!
'Twill all be past anon.
O God,
If thou wilt not have mercy on my soul,
Yet for Christ's sake, whose blood hath ransomed me,   100
Impose some end to my incessant pain.
Let Faustus live in hell a thousand years,
A hundred thousand, and at last be saved.
O, no end is limited to damnèd souls.
Why wert thou not a creature wanting soul?   105
Or why is this immortal that thou hast?
Ah, Pythagoras' *metempsychosis*, were that true,
This soul should fly from me and I be changed
Unto some brutish beast.
All beasts are happy, for, when they die,   110
Their souls are soon dissolved in elements;
But mine must live still to be plagued in hell.
Curst be the parents that engendered me!
No, Faustus, curse thyself. Curse Lucifer,
That hath deprived thee of the joys of heaven.   115

The clock striketh twelve.

O, it strikes, it strikes! Now, body, turn to air,
Or Lucifer will bear thee quick to hell.

Thunder and lightning.

O soul, be changed into little waterdrops,
And fall into the ocean, ne'er be found!
My God, my God, look not so fierce on me!   120

Enter [LUCIFER, MEPHISTOPHELES, *and other*] DEVILS.

Adders and serpents, let me breathe a while!
Ugly hell, gape not. Come not, Lucifer!
I'll burn my books. Ah, Mephistopheles!

[*The* DEVILS] *exeunt with him.*

[Epilogue]

Enter CHORUS.

CHORUS. Cut is the branch that might have grown full straight,
    And burnèd is Apollo's laurel bough
    That sometime grew within this learnèd man.
    Faustus is gone. Regard his hellish fall,
    Whose fiendful fortune may exhort the wise   5
    Only to wonder at unlawful things,
    Whose deepness doth entice such forward wits
    To practise more than heavenly power permits.

[*Exit.*]

Terminat hora diem; terminat author opus.

DOCTOR FAUSTUS: B-TEXT

Dramatis Personae

THE CHORUS.
DOCTOR JOHN FAUSTUS.
WAGNER.
GOOD ANGEL.
BAD ANGEL.
VALDES.
CORNELIUS.
THREE SCHOLARS.
LUCIFER.
DEVILS.
MEPHISTOPHELES.
ROBIN, *the Clown*.
A WOMAN DEVIL.
DICK.
BEELZEBUB.
PRIDE,
COVETOUSNESS,
ENVY,
WRATH,
GLUTTONY,
SLOTH,
LECHERY,
    the Seven Deadly Sins.
POPE ADRIAN.
RAYMOND, KING OF
    HUNGARY.
BRUNO, *the rival Pope*.
THE CARDINAL OF
    FRANCE.
THE CARDINAL OF PADUA.
THE ARCHBISHOP OF
    RHEIMS.

THE BISHOP OF
    LORRAINE.
MONKS.
FRIARS.
A VINTNER.
MARTINO.
FREDERICK.
OFFICERS.
GENTLEMEN.
BENVOLIO.
THE EMPEROR OF
    GERMANY, CHARLES V.
THE DUKE OF SAXONY.
ALEXANDER THE GREAT,
HIS PARAMOUR,
    spirits.
DARIUS.
BELIMOTH,
ASHTAROTH,
    devils.
SOLDIERS.
A HORSE-COURSER.
A CARTER.
A HOSTESS.
THE DUKE OF VANHOLT.
THE DUCHESS OF
    VANHOLT.
A SERVANT.
HELEN OF TROY, *a spirit*.
AN OLD MAN.
TWO CUPIDS.

[Prologue]

Enter CHORUS.

CHORUS. Not marching in the fields of Trasimene
　　　Where Mars did mate the warlike Carthagens,
　　　Nor sporting in the dalliance of love
　　　In courts of kings where state is overturned,
　　　Nor in the pomp of proud audacious deeds, 5
　　　Intends our muse to vaunt his heavenly verse.
　　　Only this, gentles: we must now perform
　　　The form of Faustus' fortunes, good or bad.
　　　And now to patient judgements we appeal,
　　　And speak for Faustus in his infancy. 10
　　　Now is he born, of parents base of stock,
　　　In Germany, within a town called Rhode.
　　　At riper years to Wittenberg he went,
　　　Whereas his kinsmen chiefly brought him up.
　　　So much he profits in divinity 15
　　　That shortly he was graced with doctor's name,
　　　Excelling all, and sweetly can dispute
　　　In th' heavenly matters of theology;
　　　Till, swoll'n with cunning of a self-conceit,
　　　His waxen wings did mount above his reach, 20
　　　And melting, heavens conspired his overthrow.
　　　For, falling to a devilish exercise,
　　　And glutted now with learning's golden gifts,
　　　He surfeits upon cursèd necromancy;
　　　Nothing so sweet as magic is to him, 25
　　　Which he prefers before his chiefest bliss.
　　　And this the man that in his study sits.

　　　[Exit.]

Act I

[I.i]

FAUSTUS *in his study.*

FAUSTUS. Settle thy studies, Faustus, and begin
 To sound the depth of that thou wilt profess.
 Having commenced, be a divine in show,
 Yet level at the end of every art,
 And live and die in Aristotle's works.   5
 Sweet *Analytics*, 'tis thou hast ravished me!
 [*He reads.*] *Bene disserere est finis logices.*
 Is to dispute well logic's chiefest end?
 Affords this art no greater miracle?
 Then read no more; thou hast attained that end.   10
 A greater subject fitteth Faustus' wit.
 Bid *Oeconomy* farewell, and Galen, come!
 Be a physician, Faustus. Heap up gold,
 And be eternised for some wondrous cure.
 [*He reads.*] *Summum bonum medicinae sanitas:*   15
 The end of physic is our body's health.
 Why Faustus, hast thou not attained that end?
 Are not thy bills hung up as monuments,
 Whereby whole cities have escaped the plague
 And thousand desperate maladies been cured?   20
 Yet art thou still but Faustus, and a man.
 Couldst thou make men to live eternally,
 Or, being dead, raise them to life again,
 Then this profession were to be esteemed.
 Physic, farewell! Where is Justinian?   25
 [*He reads.*] *Si una eademque res legatur duobus,*
 Alter rem, alter valorem rei, etc.
 A petty case of paltry legacies!
 [*He reads.*] *Exhaereditare filium non potest pater nisi* –

Such is the subject of the Institute   30
And universal body of the law.
This study fits a mercenary drudge
Who aims at nothing but external trash –
Too servile and illiberal for me.
When all is done, divinity is best.   35
Jerome's Bible, Faustus, view it well.
[*He reads.*] *Stipendium peccati mors est.* Ha!
Stipendium, etc.
The reward of sin is death? That's hard.
[*He reads.*] *Si peccasse negamus, fallimur*   40
Et nulla est in nobis veritas.
If we say that we have no sin,
We deceive ourselves, and there is no truth in us.
Why then belike we must sin,
And so consequently die.   45
Ay, we must die an everlasting death.
What doctrine call you this? *Che serà, serà*:
What will be, shall be. Divinity, adieu!

[*He picks up a book of magic.*]

These metaphysics of magicians
And necromantic books are heavenly,   50
Lines, circles, letters, characters –
Ay, these are those that Faustus most desires.
O, what a world of profit and delight,
Of power, of honour, and omnipotence,
Is promised to the studious artisan!   55
All things that move between the quiet poles
Shall be at my command. Emperors and kings
Are but obeyed in their several provinces,
But his dominion that exceeds in this
Stretcheth as far as doth the mind of man.   60
A sound magician is a demigod.
Here, tire my brains to get a deity.
Wagner!

Enter WAGNER.

                Commend me to my dearest friends,

The German Valdes and Cornelius.
Request them earnestly to visit me.   65

WAGNER. I will, sir.

Exit.

FAUSTUS. Their conference will be a greater help to me
Than all my labours, plod I ne'er so fast.

Enter the [GOOD] ANGEL *and* SPIRIT, [*the* BAD ANGEL].

GOOD ANGEL. O Faustus, lay that damned book aside
And gaze not on it, lest it tempt thy soul   70
And heap God's heavy wrath upon thy head!
Read, read the Scriptures. That is blasphemy.

BAD ANGEL. Go forward, Faustus, in that famous art
Wherein all nature's treasure is contained.
Be thou on earth as Jove is in the sky,   75
Lord and commander of these elements.

Exeunt ANGELS.

FAUSTUS. How am I glutted with conceit of this!
Shall I make spirits fetch me what I please?
Resolve me of all ambiguities?
Perform what desperate enterprise I will?   80
I'll have them fly to India for gold,
Ransack the ocean for orient pearl,
And search all corners of the new-found world
For pleasant fruits and princely delicates.
I'll have them read me strange philosophy   85
And tell the secrets of all foreign kings.
I'll have them wall all Germany with brass
And make swift Rhine circle fair Wittenberg.
I'll have them fill the public schools with silk,
Wherewith the students shall be bravely clad.   90
I'll levy soldiers with the coin they bring
And chase the Prince of Parma from our land,
And reign sole king of all the provinces;
Yea, stranger engines for the brunt of war
Than was the fiery keel at Antwerp bridge   95

I'll make my servile spirits to invent.
Come, German Valdes and Cornelius,
And make me blest with your sage conference!

Enter VALDES *and* CORNELIUS.

Valdes, sweet Valdes, and Cornelius,
Know that your words have won me at the last   100
To practise magic and concealèd arts.
Philosophy is odious and obscure;
Both law and physic are for petty wits;
'Tis magic, magic that hath ravished me.
Then, gentle friends, aid me in this attempt,   105
And I, that have with subtle syllogisms
Gravelled the pastors of the German Church
And made the flow'ring pride of Wittenberg
Swarm to my problems as th' infernal spirits
On sweet Musaeus when he came to hell,   110
Will be as cunning as Agrippa was,
Whose shadows made all Europe honour him.

VALDES. Faustus, these books, thy wit, and our experience
 Shall make all nations to canonise us.
 As Indian Moors obey their Spanish lords,   115
 So shall the spirits of every element
 Be always serviceable to us three.
 Like lions shall they guard us when we please,
 Like Almaine rutters with their horsemen's staves,
 Or Lapland giants, trotting by our sides;   120
 Sometimes like women, or unwedded maids,
 Shadowing more beauty in their airy brows
 Than has the white breasts of the Queen of Love.
 From Venice shall they drag huge argosies,
 And from America the golden fleece   125
 That yearly stuffed old Philip's treasury,
 If learnèd Faustus will be resolute.

FAUSTUS. Valdes, as resolute am I in this
 As thou to live. Therefore object it not.

CORNELIUS. The miracles that magic will perform   130
 Will make thee vow to study nothing else.

He that is grounded in astrology,
Enriched with tongues, well seen in minerals,
Hath all the principles magic doth require.
Then doubt not, Faustus, but to be renowned   135
And more frequented for this mystery
Than heretofore the Delphian oracle.
The spirits tell me they can dry the sea
And fetch the treasure of all foreign wrecks –
Yea, all the wealth that our forefathers hid   140
Within the massy entrails of the earth.
Then tell me, Faustus, what shall we three want?

FAUSTUS. Nothing, Cornelius. O, this cheers my soul!
Come, show me some demonstrations magical,
That I may conjure in some bushy grove   145
And have these joys in full possession.

VALDES. Then haste thee to some solitary grove,
And bear wise Bacon's and Albanus' works,
The Hebrew Psalter, and New Testament;
And whatsoever else is requisite   150
We will inform thee ere our conference cease.

CORNELIUS. Valdes, first let him know the words of art,
And then, all other ceremonies learned,
Faustus may try his cunning by himself.

VALDES. First I'll instruct thee in the rudiments, 155
And then wilt thou be perfecter than I.

FAUSTUS. Then come and dine with me, and after meat
We'll canvass every quiddity thereof,
For ere I sleep I'll try what I can do.
This night I'll conjure, though I die therefore.   160

Exeunt omnes.

[I.ii]

Enter two SCHOLARS.

FIRST SCHOLAR. I wonder what's become of Faustus, that
was wont to make our schools ring with '*sic probo*'.

Enter WAGNER, [*carrying wine*].

SECOND SCHOLAR. That shall we presently know. Here
comes his boy.

FIRST SCHOLAR. How now, sirrah, where's thy master?   5

WAGNER. God in heaven knows.

SECOND SCHOLAR. Why, dost not thou know, then?

WAGNER. Yes, I know, but that follows not.

FIRST SCHOLAR. Go to, sirrah! Leave your jesting, and tell
us where he is.   10

WAGNER. That follows not by force of argument, which
you, being licentiates, should stand upon. Therefore,
acknowledge your error, and be attentive.

SECOND SCHOLAR. Then you will not tell us?

WAGNER. You are deceived, for I will tell you. Yet if you   15
were not dunces, you would never ask me such a question.
For is he not *corpus naturale*? And is not that *mobile*? Then,
wherefore should you ask me such a question? But that
I am by nature phlegmatic, slow to wrath, and prone to
lechery – to love, I would say – it were not for you to   20
come within forty foot of the place of execution, although
I do not doubt but to see you both hanged the next
sessions. Thus, having triumphed over you, I will set my
countenance like a precisian and begin to speak thus:
Truly, my dear brethren, my master is within at dinner   25
with Valdes and Cornelius, as this wine, if it could speak,
would inform your worships. And so the Lord bless you,
preserve you, and keep you, my dear brethren.

Exit.

FIRST SCHOLAR. O Faustus,
    Then I fear that which I have long suspected,   30
    That thou art fall'n into that damnèd art
    For which they two are infamous through the world.

SECOND SCHOLAR. Were he a stranger, not allied to me,
    The danger of his soul would make me mourn.
    But come, let us go and inform the Rector.   35
    It may be his grave counsel may reclaim him.

FIRST SCHOLAR. I fear me nothing will reclaim him now.

SECOND SCHOLAR. Yet let us see what we can do.

    Exeunt.

[I.iii]

Thunder. Enter LUCIFER *and four* DEVILS [*above*], FAUSTUS
to them with this speech. [*He holds a book.*]

FAUSTUS. Now that the gloomy shadow of the night,
    Longing to view Orion's drizzling look,
    Leaps from th' Antarctic world unto the sky
    And dims the welkin with her pitchy breath,
    Faustus, begin thine incantations,   5
    And try if devils will obey thy hest,
    Seeing thou hast prayed and sacrificed to them.

    [*He draws a circle.*]

    Within this circle is Jehovah's name
    Forward and backward anagrammatised,
    Th' abbreviated names of holy saints,   10
    Figures of every adjunct to the heavens,
    And characters of signs and erring stars,
    By which the spirits are enforced to rise.
    Then fear not, Faustus, to be resolute,
    And try the utmost magic can perform.   15

    Thunder.

Sint mihi dei Acherontis propitii! Valeat numen triplex
Jehovae! Ignei, aerii, aquatici, terreni, spiritus, salvete!
Orientis princeps Lucifer, Beelzebub, inferni ardentis
monarcha, et Demogorgon, propitiamus vos, ut appareat
et surgat, Mephistopheles! Quid tu moraris? Per Jehovam,   20
Gehennam, et consecratam aquam quam nunc spargo,
signumque crucis quod nunc facio, et per vota nostra, ipse
nunc surgat nobis dicatus Mephistopheles!

[FAUSTUS *sprinkles holy water and makes a sign of the cross.*]

Enter a Devil [MEPHISTOPHELES, *in the shape of a*] *dragon.*

I charge thee to return and change thy shape.
Thou art too ugly to attend on me.   25
Go, and return an old Franciscan friar;
That holy shape becomes a devil best.

Exit Devil [MEPHISTOPHELES].

I see there's virtue in my heavenly words.
Who would not be proficient in this art?
How pliant is this Mephistopheles,   30
Full of obedience and humility!
Such is the force of magic and my spells.

Enter MEPHISTOPHELES [*disguised as a friar*].

MEPHISTOPHELES. Now, Faustus, what wouldst thou have me do?

FAUSTUS. I charge thee wait upon me whilst I live,
To do whatever Faustus shall command,   35
Be it to make the moon drop from her sphere
Or the ocean to overwhelm the world.

MEPHISTOPHELES. I am a servant to great Lucifer
And may not follow thee without his leave.
No more than he commands must we perform.   40

FAUSTUS. Did not he charge thee to appear to me?

MEPHISTOPHELES. No, I came now hither of mine own accord.

FAUSTUS. Did not my conjuring raise thee? Speak.

MEPHISTOPHELES. That was the cause, but yet *per accidens.*
    For when we hear one rack the name of God,   45
    Abjure the Scriptures and his Saviour Christ,
    We fly in hope to get his glorious soul,
    Nor will we come unless he use such means
    Whereby he is in danger to be damned.
    Therefore, the shortest cut for conjuring   50
    Is stoutly to abjure all godliness
    And pray devoutly to the prince of hell.

FAUSTUS. So Faustus hath
    Already done, and holds this principle:
    There is no chief but only Beelzebub,   55
    To whom Faustus doth dedicate himself.
    This word 'damnation' terrifies not me,
    For I confound hell in Elysium.
    My ghost be with the old philosophers!
    But leaving these vain trifles of men's souls,   60
    Tell me, what is that Lucifer, thy lord?

MEPHISTOPHELES. Arch-regent and commander of all spirits.

FAUSTUS. Was not that Lucifer an angel once?

MEPHISTOPHELES. Yes, Faustus, and most dearly loved of God.

FAUSTUS. How comes it then that he is prince of devils?   65

MEPHISTOPHELES. O, by aspiring pride and insolence,
    For which God threw him from the face of heaven.

FAUSTUS. And what are you that live with Lucifer?

MEPHISTOPHELES. Unhappy spirits that fell with Lucifer,
    Conspired against our God with Lucifer,   70
    And are for ever damned with Lucifer.

FAUSTUS. Where are you damned?

MEPHISTOPHELES. In hell.

FAUSTUS. How comes it then that thou art out of hell?

MEPHISTOPHELES. Why, this is hell, nor am I out of it.   75
    Think'st thou that I, that saw the face of God
    And tasted the eternal joys of heaven,
    Am not tormented with ten thousand hells

In being deprived of everlasting bliss?
O Faustus, leave these frivolous demands,   80
Which strikes a terror to my fainting soul!

FAUSTUS. What, is great Mephistopheles so passionate
 For being deprivèd of the joys of heaven?
 Learn thou of Faustus manly fortitude,
 And scorn those joys thou never shalt possess.   85
 Go bear these tidings to great Lucifer:
 Seeing Faustus hath incurred eternal death
 By desperate thoughts against Jove's deity,
 Say he surrenders up to him his soul,
 So he will spare him four-and-twenty years,   90
 Letting him live in all voluptuousness,
 Having thee ever to attend on me,
 To give me whatsoever I shall ask,
 To tell me whatsoever I demand,
 To slay mine enemies and to aid my friends,   95
 And always be obedient to my will.
 Go and return to mighty Lucifer,
 And meet me in my study at midnight,
 And then resolve me of thy master's mind.

MEPHISTOPHELES. I will, Faustus.   100

 Exit.

FAUSTUS. Had I as many souls as there be stars,
 I'd give them all for Mephistopheles.
 By him I'll be great emperor of the world
 And make a bridge through the moving air
 To pass the ocean; with a band of men   105
 I'll join the hills that bind the Afric shore
 And make that country continent to Spain,
 And both contributory to my crown.
 The Emperor shall not live but by my leave,
 Nor any potentate of Germany.   110
 Now that I have obtained what I desired,
 I'll live in speculation of this art
 Till Mephistopheles return again.

 Exit [FAUSTUS *below; exeunt* LUCIFER *and other* DEVILS *above*].

[I.iv]

Enter WAGNER *and* [ROBIN] *the* CLOWN.

WAGNER. Come hither, sirrah boy.

ROBIN. Boy? O disgrace to my person! Zounds, 'boy' in
your face! You have seen many boys with beards, I am
sure.

WAGNER. Sirrah, hast thou no comings in?   5

ROBIN. Yes, and goings out too, you may see, sir.

WAGNER. Alas, poor slave, see how poverty jests in his naked-
ness! I know the villain's out of service, and so hungry that
I know he would give his soul to the devil for a shoulder
of mutton, though it were blood raw.   10

ROBIN. Not so, neither. I had need to have it well roasted, and
good sauce to it, if I pay so dear, I can tell you.

WAGNER. Sirrah, wilt thou be my man and wait on me? And
I will make thee go like *Qui mihi discipulus*.

ROBIN. What, in verse?   15

WAGNER. No, slave, in beaten silk and stavesacre.

ROBIN. Stavesacre? That's good to kill vermin. Then belike
if I serve you, I shall be lousy.

WAGNER. Why, so thou shalt be, whether thou dost it or
no; for, sirrah, if thou dost not presently bind thyself to   20
me for seven years, I'll turn all the lice about thee into
familiars and make them tear thee in pieces.

ROBIN. Nay, sir, you may save yourself a labour, for they are
as familiar with me as if they paid for their meat and drink,
I can tell you.   25

WAGNER. Well, sirrah, leave your jesting, and take these
guilders. [*Offering money.*]

ROBIN. Yes, marry, sir, and I thank you, too.

WAGNER. So, now thou art to be at an hour's warning when-
soever and wheresoever the devil shall fetch thee.   30

ROBIN. Here, take your guilders. I'll none of 'em.

[*He attempts to return the money.*]

WAGNER. Not I. Thou art pressed. Prepare thyself, for I will
  presently raise up two devils to carry thee away. – Banio!
  Belcher!

ROBIN. Belcher? An Belcher come here, I'll belch him. I am   35
  not afraid of a devil.

Enter two DEVILS.

WAGNER [*to* ROBIN]. How now, sir, will you serve me now?

ROBIN. Ay, good Wagner. Take away the devil, then.

WAGNER. Spirits, away!

[*Exeunt* DEVILS.]

Now, sirrah, follow me.   40

ROBIN. I will, sir. But hark you, master, will you teach me this
  conjuring occupation?

WAGNER. Ay, sirrah, I'll teach thee to turn thyself to a dog,
  or a cat, or a mouse, or a rat, or anything.

ROBIN. A dog, or a cat, or a mouse, or a rat? O brave Wagner!   45

WAGNER. Villain, call me Master Wagner, and see that you
  walk attentively, and let your right eye be always diamet-
  rally fixed upon my left heel, that thou mayst *quasi vestigiis
  nostris insistere.*

ROBIN. Well, sir, I warrant you.   50

Exeunt.

Act II

[II.i]

Enter FAUSTUS *in his study.*

FAUSTUS. Now, Faustus, must thou needs be damned?
    Canst thou not be saved?
    What boots it then to think on God or heaven?
    Away with such vain fancies, and despair!
    Despair in God and trust in Beelzebub.   5
    Now go not backward, Faustus, be resolute.
    Why waver'st thou? O, something soundeth in mine ear:
    'Abjure this magic, turn to God again!'
    Why, he loves thee not.
    The god thou serv'st is thine own appetite,   10
    Wherein is fixed the love of Beelzebub.
    To him I'll build an altar and a church,
    And offer lukewarm blood of new-born babes.

    Enter the two ANGELS.

BAD ANGEL. Go forward, Faustus, in that famous art.

GOOD ANGEL. Sweet Faustus, leave that execrable art.   15

FAUSTUS. Contrition, prayer, repentance – what of these?

GOOD ANGEL. O, they are means to bring thee unto heaven.

BAD ANGEL. Rather illusions, fruits of lunacy,
    That make them foolish that do use them most.

GOOD ANGEL. Sweet Faustus, think of heaven and heavenly
    things.   20

BAD ANGEL. No, Faustus, think of honour and of wealth.

    Exeunt ANGELS.

FAUSTUS. Wealth?

Why, the seigniory of Emden shall be mine.
When Mephistopheles shall stand by me,
What power can hurt me? Faustus, thou art safe;   25
Cast no more doubts. Mephistopheles, come,
And bring glad tidings from great Lucifer.
Is't not midnight? Come, Mephistopheles!
Veni, veni, Mephistophile!

Enter MEPHISTOPHELES.

Now tell me what saith Lucifer thy lord.   30

MEPHISTOPHELES. That I shall wait on Faustus whilst he lives,
So he will buy my service with his soul.

FAUSTUS. Already Faustus hath hazarded that for thee.

MEPHISTOPHELES. But now thou must bequeath it solemnly
And write a deed of gift with thine own blood,   35
For that security craves Lucifer.
If thou deny it, I must back to hell.

FAUSTUS. Stay, Mephistopheles, and tell me,
What good will my soul do thy lord?

MEPHISTOPHELES. Enlarge his kingdom.   40

FAUSTUS. Is that the reason why he tempts us thus?

MEPHISTOPHELES. *Solamen miseris socios habuisse doloris.*

FAUSTUS. Why, have you any pain, that torture other?

MEPHISTOPHELES. As great as have the human souls of men.
But tell me, Faustus, shall I have thy soul?   45
And I will be thy slave, and wait on thee,
And give thee more than thou hast wit to ask.

FAUSTUS. Ay, Mephistopheles, I'll give it him.

MEPHISTOPHELES. Then, Faustus, stab thy arm courageously,
And bind thy soul that at some certain day   50
Great Lucifer may claim it as his own,
And then be thou as great as Lucifer.

FAUSTUS [*cutting his arm*]. Lo, Mephistopheles, for love of thee
Faustus hath cut his arm, and with his proper blood

Assures his soul to be great Lucifer's,   55
Chief lord and regent of perpetual night.
View here this blood that trickles from mine arm,
And let it be propitious for my wish.

MEPHISTOPHELES. But Faustus,
Write it in manner of a deed of gift.   60

FAUSTUS. Ay, so I do. [*He writes*.] But Mephistopheles,
My blood congeals, and I can write no more.

MEPHISTOPHELES. I'll fetch thee fire to dissolve it straight.

Exit.

FAUSTUS. What might the staying of my blood portend?
Is it unwilling I should write this bill?   65
Why streams it not, that I may write afresh?
'Faustus gives to thee his soul' – O, there it stayed!
Why shouldst thou not? Is not thy soul thine own?
Then write again: 'Faustus gives to thee his soul.'

Enter MEPHISTOPHELES *with the chafer of fire.*

MEPHISTOPHELES. See, Faustus, here is fire. Set it on.   70

FAUSTUS. So. Now the blood begins to clear again.
Now will I make an end immediately. [*He writes*.]

MEPHISTOPHELES [*aside*]. What will not I do to obtain his soul?

FAUSTUS. *Consummatum est*. This bill is ended,
And Faustus hath bequeathed his soul to Lucifer.   75
But what is this inscription on mine arm?
'*Homo, fuge!*' Whither should I fly?
If unto heaven, he'll throw me down to hell. –
My senses are deceived; here's nothing writ. –
O, yes, I see it plain. Even here is writ   80
'*Homo, fuge!*' Yet shall not Faustus fly.

MEPHISTOPHELES [*aside*]. I'll fetch him somewhat to delight
his mind.

Exit. Enter DEVILS, *giving crowns and rich apparel to* FAUSTUS.
They dance, and then depart. Enter MEPHISTOPHELES.

FAUSTUS. What means this show? Speak, Mephistopheles.

MEPHISTOPHELES. Nothing, Faustus, but to delight thy mind
    And let thee see what magic can perform. 85

FAUSTUS. But may I raise such spirits when I please?

MEPHISTOPHELES. Ay, Faustus, and do greater things
    than these.

FAUSTUS. Then Mephistopheles, receive this scroll,
    A deed of gift of body and of soul –
    But yet conditionally that thou perform 90
    All covenants and articles between us both.

MEPHISTOPHELES. Faustus, I swear by hell and Lucifer
    To effect all promises between us both.

FAUSTUS. Then hear me read it, Mephistopheles.

    'On these conditions following: 95

    First, that Faustus may be a spirit in form and substance.

    Secondly, that Mephistopheles shall be his servant, and
    be by him commanded.

    Thirdly, that Mephistopheles shall do for him and bring
    him whatsoever. 100

    Fourthly, that he shall be in his chamber or house
    invisible.

    Lastly, that he shall appear to the said John Faustus at
    all times in what shape and form soever he please.

    I, John Faustus of Wittenberg, Doctor, by these presents, 105
    do give both body and soul to Lucifer, Prince of the East,
    and his minister Mephistopheles; and furthermore grant
    unto them that four-and-twenty years being expired, and
    these articles above written being inviolate, full power to
    fetch or carry the said John Faustus, body and soul, flesh, 110
    blood, into their habitation wheresoever.
                           By me, John Faustus.'

MEPHISTOPHELES. Speak, Faustus. Do you deliver this
    as your deed?

FAUSTUS [*giving the deed*]. Ay. Take it, and the devil give   115
    thee good of it.

MEPHISTOPHELES. So. Now, Faustus, ask me what thou wilt.

FAUSTUS. First I will question thee about hell.
    Tell me, where is the place that men call hell?

MEPHISTOPHELES. Under the heavens.   120

FAUSTUS. Ay, so are all things else. But whereabouts?

MEPHISTOPHELES. Within the bowels of these elements,
    Where we are tortured and remain for ever.
    Hell hath no limits, nor is circumscribed
    In one self place, but where we are is hell,   125
    And where hell is there must we ever be.
    And, to be short, when all the world dissolves,
    And every creature shall be purified,
    All places shall be hell that is not heaven.

FAUSTUS. I think hell's a fable.   130

MEPHISTOPHELES. Ay, think so still, till experience change
    thy mind.

FAUSTUS. Why, dost thou think that Faustus shall be damned?

MEPHISTOPHELES. Ay, of necessity, for here's the scroll
    In which thou hast given thy soul to Lucifer.

FAUSTUS. Ay, and body too. But what of that?   135
    Think'st thou that Faustus is so fond to imagine
    That after this life there is any pain?
    No, these are trifles and mere old wives' tales.

MEPHISTOPHELES. But I am an instance to prove the contrary,
    For I tell thee I am damned and now in hell.   140

FAUSTUS. Nay, an this be hell, I'll willingly be damned.
    What? Sleeping, eating, walking, and disputing?

    But leaving this, let me have a wife, the fairest maid
    in Germany, for I am wanton and lascivious and cannot
    live without a wife.   145

MEPHISTOPHELES. Well, Faustus, thou shalt have a wife.

He fetches in a WOMAN DEVIL.

FAUSTUS. What sight is this?

MEPHISTOPHELES. Now, Faustus, wilt thou have a wife?

FAUSTUS. Here's a hot whore indeed! No, I'll no wife.

MEPHISTOPHELES. Marriage is but a ceremonial toy.   150
    An if thou lovest me, think no more of it.

    [*Exit* DEVIL.]

    I'll cull thee out the fairest courtesans
    And bring them every morning to thy bed.
    She whom thine eye shall like, thy heart shall have,
    Were she as chaste as was Penelope,   155
    As wise as Saba, or as beautiful
    As was bright Lucifer before his fall.

    [*Presenting a book.*]

    Here, take this book and peruse it well.
    The iterating of these lines brings gold;
    The framing of this circle on the ground   160
    Brings thunder, whirlwinds, storm, and lightning.
    Pronounce this thrice devoutly to thyself,
    And men in harness shall appear to thee,
    Ready to execute what thou command'st.

FAUSTUS. Thanks, Mephistopheles, for this sweet book.   165
    This will I keep as chary as my life.

    Exeunt.

[II.ii]

Enter [ROBIN] *the* CLOWN [*with a conjuring book*].

ROBIN [*calling offstage*]. What, Dick, look to the horses there
    till I come again. – I have gotten one of Doctor Faustus'
    conjuring books, and now we'll have such knavery as 't
    passes.

Enter DICK.

DICK. What, Robin, you must come away and walk the horses.   5

ROBIN. I walk the horses? I scorn 't, 'faith. I have other matters
in hand. Let the horses walk themselves an they will. [*He
reads.*] 'A' *per se* 'a'; 't', 'h', 'e', 'the'; 'o' *per se* 'o'; 'deny
orgon, gorgon'. – Keep further from me, O thou illiterate
and unlearned ostler.   10

DICK. 'Snails, what hast thou got there, a book? Why, thou
canst not tell ne'er a word on 't.

ROBIN. That thou shalt see presently. [*He draws a circle.*] Keep
out of the circle, I say, lest I send you into the hostry, with
a vengeance.   15

DICK. That's like, 'faith! You had best leave your foolery, for
an my master come he'll conjure you, 'faith.

ROBIN. My master conjure me? I'll tell thee what: an my
master come here, I'll clap as fair a pair of horns on's
head as e'er thou sawest in thy life.   20

DICK. Thou need'st not do that, for my mistress hath done it.

ROBIN. Ay, there be of us here that have waded as deep into
matters as other men, if they were disposed to talk.

DICK. A plague take you! I thought you did not sneak up and
down after her for nothing. But I prithee tell me in good   25
sadness, Robin, is that a conjuring book?

ROBIN. Do but speak what thou'lt have me to do, and I'll
do't. If thou'lt dance naked, put off thy clothes, and I'll
conjure thee about presently. Or if thou'lt go but to the
tavern with me, I'll give thee white wine, red wine, claret   30
wine, sack, muscadine, malmsey, and whippincrust, hold
belly hold, and we'll not pay one penny for it.

DICK. O brave! Prithee let's to it presently, for I am as dry as
a dog.

ROBIN. Come, then, let's away.   35

Exeunt.

[II.iii]

Enter FAUSTUS *in his study, and* MEPHISTOPHELES.

FAUSTUS. When I behold the heavens, then I repent
    And curse thee, wicked Mephistopheles,
    Because thou hast deprived me of those joys.

MEPHISTOPHELES. 'Twas thine own seeking, Faustus.
    Thank thyself.
    But think'st thou heaven is such a glorious thing? 5
    I tell thee, Faustus, it is not half so fair
    As thou or any man that breathe on earth.

FAUSTUS. How prov'st thou that?

MEPHISTOPHELES. 'Twas made for man; then he's
    more excellent.

FAUSTUS. If heaven was made for man, 'twas made for me. 10
    I will renounce this magic and repent.

    Enter the two ANGELS.

GOOD ANGEL. Faustus, repent! Yet God will pity thee.

BAD ANGEL. Thou art a spirit. God cannot pity thee.

FAUSTUS. Who buzzeth in mine ears I am a spirit?
    Be I a devil, yet God may pity me; 15
    Yea, God will pity me if I repent.

BAD ANGEL. Ay, but Faustus never shall repent.

    Exeunt ANGELS.

FAUSTUS. My heart is hardened; I cannot repent.
    Scarce can I name salvation, faith, or heaven.
    Swords, poison, halters, and envenomed steel 20
    Are laid before me to dispatch myself;
    And long ere this I should have done the deed,
    Had not sweet pleasure conquered deep despair.
    Have not I made blind Homer sing to me
    Of Alexander's love and Oenone's death? 25
    And hath not he that built the walls of Thebes

With ravishing sound of his melodious harp
Made music with my Mephistopheles?
Why should I die, then, or basely despair?
I am resolved, Faustus shall not repent.   30
Come, Mephistopheles, let us dispute again
And reason of divine astrology.
Speak. Are there many spheres above the moon?
Are all celestial bodies but one globe,
As is the substance of this centric earth?   35

MEPHISTOPHELES. As are the elements, such are the heavens,
Even from the moon unto the empyreal orb,
Mutually folded in each others' spheres,
And jointly move upon one axletree,
Whose terminè is termed the world's wide pole.   40
Nor are the names of Saturn, Mars, or Jupiter
Feigned, but are erring stars.

FAUSTUS. But have they all one motion, both *situ et tempore?*

MEPHISTOPHELES. All move from east to west in four-and-
twenty hours upon the poles of the world, but differ in their   45
motions upon the poles of the zodiac.

FAUSTUS. These slender questions Wagner can decide.
Hath Mephistopheles no greater skill?
Who knows not the double motion of the planets?
That the first is finished in a natural day,   50
The second thus: Saturn in thirty years,
Jupiter in twelve, Mars in four, the sun, Venus, and
Mercury in a year, the moon in twenty-eight days. These
are freshmen's questions. But tell me, hath every sphere a
dominion or *intelligentia?*   55

MEPHISTOPHELES. Ay.

FAUSTUS. How many heavens or spheres are there?

MEPHISTOPHELES. Nine: the seven planets, the firmament,
and the empyreal heaven.

FAUSTUS. But is there not *coelum igneum et crystallinum?*   60

MEPHISTOPHELES. No, Faustus, they be but fables.

FAUSTUS. Resolve me then in this one question: why are
    not conjunctions, oppositions, aspects, eclipses all at one
    time, but in some years we have more, in some less?

MEPHISTOPHELES. *Per inaequalem motum respectu totius.*   65

FAUSTUS. Well, I am answered. Now tell me who made the world.

MEPHISTOPHELES. I will not.

FAUSTUS. Sweet Mephistopheles, tell me.

MEPHISTOPHELES. Move me not, Faustus.   70

FAUSTUS. Villain, have not I bound thee to tell me anything?

MEPHISTOPHELES. Ay, that is not against our kingdom.
    This is. Thou art damned. Think thou of hell.

FAUSTUS. Think, Faustus, upon God, that made the world.

MEPHISTOPHELES. Remember this.   75

    Exit.

FAUSTUS. Ay, go, accursèd spirit, to ugly hell!
    'Tis thou hast damned distressèd Faustus' soul.
    Is 't not too late?

    Enter the two ANGELS.

BAD ANGEL. Too late.

GOOD ANGEL. Never too late, if Faustus will repent.   80

BAD ANGEL. If thou repent, devils will tear thee in pieces.

GOOD ANGEL. Repent, and they shall never raze thy skin.

    Exeunt ANGELS.

FAUSTUS. O Christ, my Saviour, my Saviour,
    Help to save distressèd Faustus' soul!

    Enter LUCIFER, BEELZEBUB, *and* MEPHISTOPHELES.

LUCIFER. Christ cannot save thy soul, for he is just.   85
    There's none but I have interest in the same.

FAUSTUS. O, what art thou that look'st so terribly?

LUCIFER. I am Lucifer,
    And this is my companion prince in hell.

FAUSTUS. O, Faustus, they are come to fetch thy soul!   90

BEELZEBUB. We are come to tell thee thou dost injure us.

LUCIFER. Thou call'st on Christ, contrary to thy promise.

BEELZEBUB. Thou shouldst not think on God.

LUCIFER. Think on the devil.

BEELZEBUB. And his dam, too.   95

FAUSTUS. Nor will Faustus henceforth. Pardon him for this,
    and Faustus vows never to look to heaven.

LUCIFER. So shalt thou show thyself an obedient servant,
    and we will highly gratify thee for it.

BEELZEBUB. Faustus, we are come from hell in person to   100
    show thee some pastime. Sit down, and thou shalt behold
    the Seven Deadly Sins appear to thee in their own proper
    shapes and likeness.

FAUSTUS. That sight will be as pleasant to me as paradise
    was to Adam the first day of his creation.   105

LUCIFER. Talk not of paradise or creation, but mark the show.
    Go, Mephistopheles, fetch them in.

    [FAUSTUS *sits*. MEPHISTOPHELES *fetches the* SINS.]

    Enter the SEVEN DEADLY SINS.

BEELZEBUB. Now, Faustus, question them of their names
    and dispositions.

FAUSTUS. That shall I soon. – What art thou, the first?   110

PRIDE. I am Pride. I disdain to have any parents. I am like
    to Ovid's flea: I can creep into every corner of a wench.
    Sometimes like a periwig I sit upon her brow; next, like
    a necklace I hang about her neck; then, like a fan of
    feathers I kiss her, and then, turning myself to a wrought   115
    smock, do what I list. But fie, what a smell is here! I'll

not speak a word more for a king's ransom, unless the
ground be perfumed and covered with cloth of arras.

FAUSTUS. Thou art a proud knave, indeed. – What art thou,
the second?   120

COVETOUSNESS. I am Covetousness, begotten of an old
churl in a leather bag; and might I now obtain my wish,
this house, you, and all should turn to gold, that I might
lock you safe into my chest. O my sweet gold!

FAUSTUS. And what art thou, the third?   125

ENVY. I am Envy, begotten of a chimney-sweeper and an
oyster-wife. I cannot read, and therefore wish all books
burnt. I am lean with seeing others eat. O, that there
would come a famine over all the world, that all might
die and I live alone! Then thou shouldst see how fat I'd   130
be. But must thou sit and I stand? Come down, with a
vengeance!

FAUSTUS. Out, envious wretch! – But what art thou, the
fourth?

WRATH. I am Wrath. I had neither father nor mother. I   135
leaped out of a lion's mouth when I was scarce an hour old,
and ever since have run up and down the world with these
case of rapiers, wounding myself when I could get none
to fight withal. I was born in hell, and look to it, for some
of you shall be my father.   140

FAUSTUS. And what art thou, the fifth?

GLUTTONY. I am Gluttony. My parents are all dead, and
the devil a penny they have left me but a small pension, and
that buys me thirty meals a day, and ten bevers – a small
trifle to suffice nature. I come of a royal pedigree. My   145
father was a gammon of bacon, and my mother was a
hogshead of claret wine. My godfathers were these: Peter
Pickled-herring and Martin Martlemas-beef. But my godmother, O, she was an ancient gentlewoman; her name
was Margery March-beer. Now, Faustus, thou hast   150
heard all my progeny, wilt thou bid me to supper?

FAUSTUS. Not I.

GLUTTONY. Then the devil choke thee!

FAUSTUS. Choke thyself, glutton! – What art thou, the sixth?

SLOTH. Heigh-ho. I am Sloth. I was begotten on a sunny bank.
155 Heigh-ho. I'll not speak a word more for a king's ransom.

FAUSTUS. And what are you, Mistress Minx, the seventh
and last?

LECHERY. Who, I? I, sir? I am one that loves an inch of raw
mutton better than an ell of fried stockfish, and the first   160
letter of my name begins with lechery.

LUCIFER. Away, to hell, away! On, piper!

Exeunt the SEVEN SINS.

FAUSTUS. O, how this sight doth delight my soul!

LUCIFER. But Faustus, in hell is all manner of delight.

FAUSTUS. O, might I see hell and return again safe, how   165
happy were I then!

LUCIFER. Faustus, thou shalt. At midnight I will send for
thee. [*Presenting a book.*] Meanwhile, peruse this book, and
view it throughly, and thou shalt turn thyself into what
shape thou wilt.   170

FAUSTUS [*taking the book*]. Thanks, mighty Lucifer.
This will I keep as chary as my life.

LUCIFER. Now, Faustus, farewell.

FAUSTUS. Farewell, great Lucifer. Come, Mephistopheles.

Exeunt omnes, several ways.

Act III

[III.Chorus]

Enter the CHORUS.

CHORUS. Learnèd Faustus,
    To find the secrets of astronomy
    Graven in the book of Jove's high firmament,
    Did mount him up to scale Olympus' top,
    Where, sitting in a chariot burning bright   5
    Drawn by the strength of yokèd dragons' necks,
    He views the clouds, the planets, and the stars,
    The tropics, zones, and quarters of the sky,
    From the bright circle of the hornèd moon
    Even to the height of *Primum Mobile;*   10
    And, whirling round with this circumference
    Within the concave compass of the pole,
    From east to west his dragons swiftly glide
    And in eight days did bring him home again.
    Not long he stayed within his quiet house   15
    To rest his bones after his weary toil,
    But new exploits do hale him out again,
    And, mounted then upon a dragon's back,
    That with his wings did part the subtle air,
    He now is gone to prove cosmography,   20
    That measures coasts and kingdoms of the earth,
    And, as I guess, will first arrive at Rome
    To see the Pope and manner of his court
    And take some part of holy Peter's feast,
    The which this day is highly solemnised.   25

    Exit.

[III.i]

Enter FAUSTUS *and* MEPHISTOPHELES.

FAUSTUS. Having now, my good Mephistopheles,
    Passed with delight the stately town of Trier,
    Environed round with airy mountain-tops,
    With walls of flint and deep intrenchèd lakes,
    Not to be won by any conquering prince;   5
    From Paris next, coasting the realm of France,
    We saw the river Maine fall into Rhine,
    Whose banks are set with groves of fruitful vines.
    Then up to Naples, rich Campania,
    Whose buildings, fair and gorgeous to the eye,   10
    The streets straight forth and paved with finest brick.
    There saw we learnèd Maro's golden tomb,
    The way he cut an English mile in length
    Through a rock of stone in one night's space.
    From thence to Venice, Padua, and the east,   15
    In one of which a sumptuous temple stands
    That threats the stars with her aspiring top,
    Whose frame is paved with sundry coloured stones,
    And roofed aloft with curious work in gold.
    Thus hitherto hath Faustus spent his time.   20
    But tell me now, what resting place is this?
    Hast thou, as erst I did command,
    Conducted me within the walls of Rome?

MEPHISTOPHELES. I have, my Faustus, and for proof thereof
    This is the goodly palace of the Pope;   25
    And 'cause we are no common guests
    I choose his privy chamber for our use.

FAUSTUS. I hope his Holiness will bid us welcome.

MEPHISTOPHELES. All's one, for we'll be bold with his venison.
    But now, my Faustus, that thou mayst perceive   30
    What Rome contains for to delight thine eyes,
    Know that this city stands upon seven hills
    That underprop the groundwork of the same.
    Just through the midst runs flowing Tiber's stream,
    With winding banks that cut it in two parts,   35

Over the which two stately bridges lean,
That make safe passage to each part of Rome.
Upon the bridge called Ponte Angelo
Erected is a castle passing strong,
Where thou shalt see such store of ordnance   40
As that the double cannons, forged of brass,
Do match the number of the days contained
Within the compass of one complete year –
Beside the gates and high pyramides
That Julius Caesar brought from Africa.   45

FAUSTUS. Now, by the kingdoms of infernal rule,
    Of Styx, of Acheron, and the fiery lake
    Of ever-burning Phlegethon, I swear
    That I do long to see the monuments
    And situation of bright splendent Rome.   50
    Come, therefore, let's away!

MEPHISTOPHELES. Nay stay, my Faustus. I know you'd
        see the Pope
    And take some part of holy Peter's feast,
    The which this day with high solemnity
    This day is held through Rome and Italy   55
    In honour of the Pope's triumphant victory.

FAUSTUS. Sweet Mephistopheles, thou pleasest me.
    Whilst I am here on earth, let me be cloyed
    With all things that delight the heart of man.
    My four-and-twenty years of liberty   60
    I'll spend in pleasure and in dalliance,
    That Faustus' name, whilst this bright frame doth stand,
    May be admirèd through the furthest land.

MEPHISTOPHELES. 'Tis well said, Faustus. Come, then,
        stand by me,
    And thou shalt see them come immediately.   65

FAUSTUS. Nay, stay, my gentle Mephistopheles,
    And grant me my request, and then I go.
    Thou know'st within the compass of eight days
    We viewed the face of heaven, of earth, and hell.
    So high our dragons soared into the air   70

That, looking down, the earth appeared to me
No bigger than my hand in quantity.
There did we view the kingdoms of the world,
And what might please mine eye I there beheld.
Then in this show let me an actor be,   75
That this proud Pope may Faustus' cunning see.

MEPHISTOPHELES. Let it be so, my Faustus. But first stay
   And view their triumphs as they pass this way,
   And then devise what best contents thy mind,
   By cunning in thine art, to cross the Pope   80
   Or dash the pride of this solemnity –
   To make his monks and abbots stand like apes
   And point like antics at his triple crown,
   To beat the beads about the friars' pates
   Or clap huge horns upon the cardinals' heads,   85
   Or any villainy thou canst devise,
   And I'll perform it, Faustus. Hark, they come.
   This day shall make thee be admired in Rome.

   [*They stand aside.*]

   Enter the CARDINALS [*of France and Padua*] *and* BISHOPS
   [*of Lorraine and Rheims*], *some bearing crosiers, some the pillars;*
   MONKS *and* FRIARS *singing their procession. Then the* POPE
   [ADRIAN] *and* RAYMOND, KING OF HUNGARY, *with*
   BRUNO [*the rival Pope*] *led in chains.* [BRUNO'*s papal crown is*
   borne in.]

POPE. Cast down our footstool.

RAYMOND.   Saxon Bruno, stoop,
   Whilst on thy back his Holiness ascends   90
   Saint Peter's chair and state pontifical.

BRUNO. Proud Lucifer, that state belongs to me!
   But thus I fall to Peter, not to thee.

   [*He kneels in front of the throne.*]

POPE. To me and Peter shalt thou grovelling lie
   And crouch before the papal dignity.   95
   Sound trumpets, then, for thus Saint Peter's heir
   From Bruno's back ascends Saint Peter's chair.

A flourish while he ascends.

Thus, as the gods creep on with feet of wool
Long ere with iron hands they punish men,
So shall our sleeping vengeance now arise   100
And smite with death thy hated enterprise.
Lord Cardinals of France and Padua,
Go forthwith to our holy consistory
And read amongst the statutes decretal
What, by the holy council held at Trent,   105
The sacred synod hath decreed for him
That doth assume the papal government
Without election and a true consent.
Away, and bring us word with speed.

FIRST CARDINAL. We go, my lord.   110

   Exeunt CARDINALS.

POPE. Lord Raymond –

   [POPE ADRIAN *and* RAYMOND *converse apart.*]

FAUSTUS [*aside*]. Go haste thee, gentle Mephistopheles.
Follow the cardinals to the consistory,
And as they turn their superstitious books
Strike them with sloth and drowsy idleness,   115
And make them sleep so sound that in their shapes
Thyself and I may parley with this Pope,
This proud confronter of the Emperor,
And in despite of all his holiness
Restore this Bruno to his liberty   120
And bear him to the states of Germany.

MEPHISTOPHELES. Faustus, I go.

FAUSTUS. Dispatch it soon.
The Pope shall curse that Faustus came to Rome.

   Exeunt FAUSTUS *and* MEPHISTOPHELES.

BRUNO. Pope Adrian, let me have some right of law.   125
I was elected by the Emperor.

POPE. We will depose the Emperor for that deed

And curse the people that submit to him.
Both he and thou shalt stand excommunicate
And interdict from Church's privilege   130
And all society of holy men.
He grows too proud in his authority,
Lifting his lofty head above the clouds,
And like a steeple overpeers the Church.
But we'll pull down his haughty insolence.   135
And as Pope Alexander, our progenitor,
Trod on the neck of German Frederick,
Adding this golden sentence to our praise,
'That Peter's heirs should tread on emperors
And walk upon the dreadful adder's back,   140
Treading the lion and the dragon down,
And fearless spurn the killing basilisk',
So will we quell that haughty schismatic
And by authority apostolical
Depose him from his regal government.   145

BRUNO. Pope Julius swore to princely Sigismund,
For him and the succeeding popes of Rome,
To hold the emperors their lawful lords.

POPE. Pope Julius did abuse the Church's rights,
And therefore none of his decrees can stand.   150
Is not all power on earth bestowed on us?
And therefore, though we would, we cannot err.
Behold this silver belt, whereto is fixed
Seven golden keys fast sealed with seven seals
In token of our sevenfold power from heaven,   155
To bind or loose, lock fast, condemn, or judge,
Resign, or seal, or whatso pleaseth us.
Then he and thou and all the world shall stoop,
Or be assurèd of our dreadful curse
To light as heavy as the pains of hell.   160

Enter FAUSTUS *and* MEPHISTOPHELES, [*dressed*] *like
the cardinals.*

MEPHISTOPHELES [*aside*]. Now tell me, Faustus, are we
    not fitted well?

FAUSTUS [*aside*]. Yes, Mephistopheles, and two such cardinals
    Ne'er served a holy pope as we shall do.
    But whilst they sleep within the consistory,
    Let us salute his reverend Fatherhood.   165

RAYMOND [*to the* POPE]. Behold, my lord, the cardinals
    are returned.

POPE. Welcome, grave fathers. Answer presently:
    What have our holy council there decreed
    Concerning Bruno and the Emperor,
    In quittance of their late conspiracy   170
    Against our state and papal dignity?

FAUSTUS. Most sacred patron of the Church of Rome,
    By full consent of all the synod
    Of priests and prelates, it is thus decreed:
    That Bruno and the German Emperor   175
    Be held as Lollards and bold schismatics
    And proud disturbers of the Church's peace.
    And if that Bruno by his own assent,
    Without enforcement of the German peers,
    Did seek to wear the triple diadem   180
    And by your death to climb Saint Peter's chair,
    The statutes decretal have thus decreed:
    He shall be straight condemned of heresy
    And on a pile of faggots burnt to death.

POPE. It is enough. Here, take him to your charge,   185
    And bear him straight to Ponte Angelo,
    And in the strongest tower enclose him fast.
    Tomorrow, sitting in our consistory
    With all our college of grave cardinals,
    We will determine of his life or death.   190
    Here, take his triple crown along with you
    And leave it in the Church's treasury.

    [BRUNO's *papal crown is given to* FAUSTUS *and*
    MEPHISTOPHELES.]

    Make haste again, my good lord cardinals,
    And take our blessing apostolical.

MEPHISTOPHELES [*aside*]. So, so, was never devil thus
    blest before! 195

FAUSTUS [*aside*]. Away, sweet Mephistopheles, begone.
    The cardinals will be plagued for this anon.

    Exeunt FAUSTUS *and* MEPHISTOPHELES [*with* BRUNO].

POPE. Go presently and bring a banquet forth,
    That we may solemnise Saint Peter's feast
    And with Lord Raymond, King of Hungary, 200
    Drink to our late and happy victory.

    Exeunt.

[III.ii]

*A sennet while the banquet is brought in. [Seats are provided at the
banquet. Exeunt* ATTENDANTS,] *and then enter* FAUSTUS *and*
MEPHISTOPHELES *in their own shapes.*

MEPHISTOPHELES. Now, Faustus, come prepare thyself for mirth.
    The sleepy cardinals are hard at hand
    To censure Bruno, that is posted hence
    And on a proud-paced steed, as swift as thought,
    Flies o'er the Alps to fruitful Germany, 5
    There to salute the woeful Emperor.

FAUSTUS. The Pope will curse them for their sloth today,
    That slept both Bruno and his crown away.
    But now, that Faustus may delight his mind
    And by their folly make some merriment, 10
    Sweet Mephistopheles, so charm me here
    That I may walk invisible to all
    And do whate'er I please, unseen of any.

MEPHISTOPHELES. Faustus, thou shalt. Then kneel down
    presently,

    [FAUSTUS *kneels.*]

    Whilst on thy head I lay my hand
    And charm thee with this magic wand. 15

[*Presenting a magic girdle.*]

> First wear this girdle; then appear
> Invisible to all are here.
> The planets seven, the gloomy air,
> Hell, and the Furies' forkèd hair,   20
> Pluto's blue fire, and Hecate's tree
> With magic spells so compass thee
> That no eye may thy body see.

[FAUSTUS *rises.*]

> So, Faustus, now, for all their holiness,
> Do what thou wilt, thou shalt not be discerned.   25

FAUSTUS. Thanks, Mephistopheles. Now, friars, take heed
   Lest Faustus make your shaven crowns to bleed.

MEPHISTOPHELES. Faustus, no more. See where the
      cardinals come.

Enter POPE *and all the lords:* [RAYMOND, *King of Hungary, the*
ARCHBISHOP OF RHEIMS, *etc.,* FRIARS *and* ATTEN-
DANTS.] *Enter the* [*two*] CARDINALS [*of France and Padua*]
with a book.

POPE. Welcome, lord cardinals. Come sit down.

[*They sit.*]

> Lord Raymond, take your seat. Friars, attend,   30
> And see that all things be in readiness,
> As best beseems this solemn festival.

FIRST CARDINAL. First, may it please your sacred Holiness
   To view the sentence of the reverend synod
   Concerning Bruno and the Emperor?   35

POPE. What needs this question? Did I not tell you
   Tomorrow we would sit i' th' consistory
   And there determine of his punishment?
   You brought us word even now, it was decreed
   That Bruno and the cursèd Emperor   40
   Were by the holy council both condemned
   For loathèd Lollards and base schismatics.
   Then wherefore would you have me view that book?

FIRST CARDINAL. Your Grace mistakes. You gave us no
    such charge.

RAYMOND. Deny it not. We all are witnesses   45
    That Bruno here was late delivered you,
    With his rich triple crown to be reserved
    And put into the Church's treasury.

BOTH CARDINALS. By holy Paul, we saw them not.

POPE. By Peter, you shall die   50
    Unless you bring them forth immediately. –
    Hale them to prison. Lade their limbs with gyves! –
    False prelates, for this hateful treachery
    Curst be your souls to hellish misery.

    [*Exeunt* ATTENDANTS *with the two* CARDINALS.]

FAUSTUS [*aside*]. So, they are safe. Now, Faustus, to the feast.   55
    The Pope had never such a frolic guest.

POPE. Lord Archbishop of Rheims, sit down with us.

ARCHBISHOP [*sitting*]. I thank your Holiness.

FAUSTUS. Fall to. The devil choke you an you spare.

POPE. Who's that spoke? Friars, look about.   60
    Lord Raymond, pray fall to. I am beholding
    To the Bishop of Milan for this so rare a present.

FAUSTUS [*snatching the meat*]. I thank you, sir.

POPE. How now? Who snatched the meat from me?
    Villains, why speak you not? –   65
    My good Lord Archbishop, here's a most dainty dish
    Was sent me from a Cardinal in France.

FAUSTUS [*snatching the dish*]. I'll have that, too.

POPE. What Lollards do attend our Holiness,
    That we receive such great indignity?   70
    Fetch me some wine.

    [*Wine is brought.*]

FAUSTUS [*aside*]. Ay, pray do, for Faustus is adry.

POPE. Lord Raymond, I drink unto your Grace.

FAUSTUS [*snatching the cup*]. I pledge your Grace.

POPE. My wine gone, too? Ye lubbers, look about   75
    And find the man that doth this villainy,
    Or by our sanctitude you all shall die! –
    I pray, my lords, have patience at this troublesome banquet.

ARCHBISHOP. Please it your Holiness, I think it be some   80
    ghost crept out of purgatory and now is come unto your
    Holiness for his pardon.

POPE. It may be so.
    Go, then, command our priests to sing a dirge
    To lay the fury of this same troublesome ghost.   85

    [*Exit one. The* POPE *crosses himself.*]

FAUSTUS. How now? Must every bit be spicèd with a cross?

    [*The* POPE *crosses himself again.*]

    Nay, then, take that!

    [FAUSTUS *gives the* POPE *a blow on the head.*]

POPE. O, I am slain! Help me, my lords.
    O, come and help to bear my body hence.
    Damned be this soul for ever for this deed!   90

    Exeunt the POPE *and his train.*

MEPHISTOPHELES. Now, Faustus, what will you do now? For
    I can tell you you'll be cursed with bell, book, and candle.

FAUSTUS. Bell, book, and candle; candle, book, and bell,
    Forward and backward, to curse Faustus to hell.

    Enter the FRIARS *with bell, book, and candle, for the dirge.*

FIRST FRIAR. Come, brethren, let's about our business with   95
    good devotion.

    [*The* FRIARS *chant.*]

    Cursèd be he that stole his Holiness' meat from the table.
        Maledicat Dominus!

Cursèd be he that struck his Holiness a blow on the face.
   Maledicat Dominus!   100
Cursèd be he that struck Friar Sandelo a blow on the pate.
   Maledicat Dominus!
Cursèd be he that disturbeth our holy dirge.
   Maledicat Dominus!
Cursèd be he that took away his Holiness' wine.   105
   Maledicat Dominus!

[FAUSTUS *and* MEPHISTOPHELES] *beat the* FRIARS,
fling firework among them, and exeunt.

[III.iii]

Enter CLOWN [ROBIN], *and* DICK *with a cup.*

DICK. Sirrah Robin, we were best look that your devil can
   answer the stealing of this same cup, for the Vintner's
   boy follows us at the hard heels.

ROBIN. 'Tis no matter. Let him come. An he follow us, I'll
   so conjure him as he was never conjured in his life, warrant   5
   him. Let me see the cup.

Enter VINTNER.

DICK [*giving the cup to* ROBIN]. Here 'tis. Yonder he comes.
   Now, Robin, now or never show thy cunning.

VINTNER. O, are you here? I am glad I have found you. You
   are a couple of fine companions! Pray, where's the cup you   10
   stole from the tavern?

ROBIN. How, how? We steal a cup? Take heed what you say.
   We look not like cup-stealers, I can tell you.

VINTNER. Never deny 't, for I know you have it, and I'll
   search you.   15

ROBIN. Search me? Ay, and spare not. [*Aside to* DICK, *giving
   him the cup.*] Hold the cup, Dick. [*To the* VINTNER.] Come,
   come, search me, search me.

[*The* VINTNER *searches* ROBIN.]

VINTNER [*to* DICK]. Come on, sirrah, let me search you now.

DICK. Ay, ay, do, do. [*Aside to* ROBIN, *giving him the cup.*]   20
    Hold the cup, Robin. [*To the* VINTNER.] I fear not your
    searching. We scorn to steal your cups, I can tell you.

[*The* VINTNER *searches* DICK.]

VINTNER. Never outface me for the matter, for sure the cup
    is between you two.

ROBIN [*brandishing the cup*]. Nay, there you lie. 'Tis beyond   25
    us both.

VINTNER. A plague take you! I thought 'twas your knavery
    to take it away. Come, give it me again.

ROBIN. Ay, much! When, can you tell? Dick, make me
    a circle, and stand close at my back, and stir not for   30
    thy life. [DICK *makes a circle.*] Vintner, you shall have
    your cup anon. Say nothing, Dick. 'O' *per se* 'O',
    Demogorgon, Belcher, and Mephistopheles!

Enter MEPHISTOPHELES. [*Exit the* VINTNER, *running.*]

MEPHISTOPHELES. You princely legions of infernal rule,
    How am I vexèd by these villains' charms!   35
    From Constantinople have they brought me now
    Only for pleasure of these damnèd slaves.

ROBIN. By Lady, sir, you have had a shrewd journey of it.
    Will it please you to take a shoulder of mutton to supper
    and a tester in your purse, and go back again?   40

DICK. Ay, I pray you heartily, sir, for we called you but in
    jest, I promise you.

MEPHISTOPHELES. To purge the rashness of this cursèd deed,
    [*To* DICK.] First, be thou turnèd to this ugly shape,
    For apish deeds transformèd to an ape.   45

ROBIN. O brave, an ape! I pray, sir, let me have the carrying
    of him about to show some tricks.

MEPHISTOPHELES. And so thou shalt. Be thou transformed
to a dog, and carry him upon thy back. Away, begone!

ROBIN. A dog? That's excellent. Let the maids look well to   50
their porridge pots, for I'll into the kitchen presently.
Come, Dick, come.

Exeunt the two CLOWNS [*with* DICK *on* ROBIN's *back*].

MEPHISTOPHELES. Now with the flames of ever-burning fire
I'll wing myself and forthwith fly amain
Unto my Faustus, to the Great Turk's court.   55

Exit.

Act IV

[IV.i]

Enter MARTINO *and* FREDERICK [*with other* OFFICERS *and* GENTLEMEN] *at several doors.*

MARTINO. What ho, officers, gentlemen!
    Hie to the presence to attend the Emperor.
    Good Frederick, see the rooms be voided straight;
    His Majesty is coming to the hall.
    Go back, and see the state in readiness.   5

    [*Exeunt some.*]

FREDERICK. But where is Bruno, our elected pope,
    That on a Fury's back came post from Rome?
    Will not his Grace consort the Emperor?

MARTINO. O, yes, and with him comes the German conjurer,
    The learnèd Faustus, fame of Wittenberg,   10
    The wonder of the world for magic art;
    And he intends to show great Carolus
    The race of all his stout progenitors,
    And bring in presence of his Majesty
    The royal shapes and warlike semblances   15
    Of Alexander and his beauteous paramour.

FREDERICK. Where is Benvolio?

MARTINO. Fast asleep, I warrant you.
    He took his rouse with stoups of Rhenish wine
    So kindly yesternight to Bruno's health   20
    That all this day the sluggard keeps his bed.

FREDERICK. See, see, his window's ope. We'll call to him.

MARTINO. What ho, Benvolio!

Enter BENVOLIO *above at a window, in his nightcap, buttoning.*

BENVOLIO. What a devil ail you two?

MARTINO. Speak softly, sir, lest the devil hear you;   25
  For Faustus at the court is late arrived,
  And at his heels a thousand Furies wait
  To accomplish whatsoever the doctor please.

BENVOLIO. What of this?

MARTINO. Come, leave thy chamber first, and thou shalt see   30
  This conjurer perform such rare exploits
  Before the Pope and royal Emperor
  As never yet was seen in Germany.

BENVOLIO. Has not the Pope enough of conjuring yet?
  He was upon the devil's back late enough;   35
  An if he be so far in love with him,
  I would he would post with him to Rome again.

FREDERICK. Speak, wilt thou come and see this sport?

BENVOLIO.   Not I.

MARTINO. Wilt thou stand in thy window and see it, then?

BENVOLIO. Ay, an I fall not asleep i' th' meantime.   40

MARTINO. The Emperor is at hand, who comes to see
  What wonders by black spells may compassed be.

BENVOLIO. Well, go you attend the Emperor. I am content
  for this once to thrust my head out at a window, for they
  say if a man be drunk overnight the devil cannot hurt him   45
  in the morning. If that be true, I have a charm in my head
  shall control him as well as the conjurer, I warrant you.

Exeunt [FREDERICK *and* MARTINO. BENVOLIO *remains
at his window.*].

A sennet. [*Enter*] *Charles the German* EMPEROR, BRUNO,
[*the Duke of*] SAXONY, FAUSTUS, MEPHISTOPHELES,
FREDERICK, MARTINO, *and* ATTENDANTS. [*The*
EMPEROR *sits in his throne.*]

EMPEROR. Wonder of men, renowned magician,
    Thrice-learnèd Faustus, welcome to our court.
    This deed of thine, in setting Bruno free   50
    From his and our professèd enemy,
    Shall add more excellence unto thine art
    Than if by powerful necromantic spells
    Thou couldst command the world's obedience.
    For ever be beloved of Carolus.   55
    And if this Bruno thou hast late redeemed
    In peace possess the triple diadem
    And sit in Peter's chair, despite of chance,
    Thou shalt be famous through all Italy
    And honoured of the German Emperor.   60

FAUSTUS. These gracious words, most royal Carolus,
    Shall make poor Faustus to his utmost power
    Both love and serve the German Emperor
    And lay his life at holy Bruno's feet.
    For proof whereof, if so your Grace be pleased,   65
    The doctor stands prepared by power of art
    To cast his magic charms, that shall pierce through
    The ebon gates of ever-burning hell
    And hale the stubborn Furies from their caves
    To compass whatsoe'er your Grace commands.   70

BENVOLIO [aside, at the window]. Blood, he speaks terribly.
    But for all that, I do not greatly believe him. He looks as
    like a conjurer as the Pope to a costermonger.

EMPEROR. Then, Faustus, as thou late didst promise us,
    We would behold that famous conqueror   75
    Great Alexander and his paramour
    In their true shapes and state majestical,
    That we may wonder at their excellence.

FAUSTUS. Your Majesty shall see them presently. –
    [Aside to MEPHISTOPHELES.] Mephistopheles, away,   80
    And with a solemn noise of trumpet's sound
    Present before this royal Emperor
    Great Alexander and his beauteous paramour.

MEPHISTOPHELES [aside to FAUSTUS]. Faustus, I will.

[*Exit.*]

BENVOLIO [*at the window*]. Well, Master Doctor, an your   85
    devils come not away quickly, you shall have me asleep
    presently. Zounds, I could eat myself for anger to think
    I have been such an ass all this while, to stand gaping
    after the devil's governor and can see nothing.

FAUSTUS [*aside*]. I'll make you feel something anon, if my   90
    art fail me not. –

    [*To* EMPEROR.] My lord, I must forewarn your Majesty
    That when my spirits present the royal shapes
    Of Alexander and his paramour,
    Your Grace demand no questions of the king,   95
    But in dumb silence let them come and go.

EMPEROR. Be it as Faustus please. We are content.

BENVOLIO [*at the window*]. Ay, ay, and I am content too.
    An thou bring Alexander and his paramour before the
    Emperor, I'll be Actaeon and turn myself to a stag.   100

FAUSTUS [*aside*]. And I'll play Diana and send you the
    horns presently.

    [*Enter* MEPHISTOPHELES.] *A sennet. Enter at one* [*door*]
    the Emperor ALEXANDER, *at the other* DARIUS. *They*
    meet; DARIUS *is thrown down.* ALEXANDER *kills him, takes*
    off his crown, and, offering to go out, his PARAMOUR *meets*
    him. He embraceth her and sets DARIUS's *crown upon her head;*
    and, coming back, both salute the [*German*] EMPEROR, *who,*
    leaving his state, offers to embrace them, which FAUSTUS *seeing*
    suddenly stays him. Then trumpets cease and music sounds.

    My gracious lord, you do forget yourself.
    These are but shadows, not substantial.

EMPEROR. O, pardon me. My thoughts are so ravishèd   105
    With sight of this renownèd emperor
    That in mine arms I would have compassed him.
    But Faustus, since I may not speak to them
    To satisfy my longing thoughts at full,
    Let me this tell thee: I have heard it said   110

That this fair lady, whilst she lived on earth,
Had on her neck a little wart or mole.
How may I prove that saying to be true?

FAUSTUS. Your Majesty may boldly go and see.

EMPEROR [*making an inspection*]. Faustus, I see it plain,   115
  And in this sight thou better pleasest me
  Than if I gained another monarchy.

FAUSTUS [*to the spirits*]. Away, begone!

  Exit Show.

  See, see, my gracious lord, what strange beast is yon, that
  thrusts his head out at window.   120

  [BENVOLIO *is seen to have sprouted horns.*]

EMPEROR. O wondrous sight! See, Duke of Saxony,
  Two spreading horns most strangely fastenèd
  Upon the head of young Benvolio.

SAXONY. What, is he asleep, or dead?

FAUSTUS. He sleeps, my lord, but dreams not of his horns.   125

EMPEROR. This sport is excellent. We'll call and wake him. –
  What ho, Benvolio!

BENVOLIO. A plague upon you! Let me sleep a while.

EMPEROR. I blame thee not to sleep much, having such a
  head of thine own.   130

SAXONY. Look up, Benvolio. 'Tis the Emperor calls.

BENVOLIO. The Emperor? Where? O, zounds, my head!

EMPEROR. Nay, an thy horns hold, 'tis no matter for thy
  head, for that's armed sufficiently.

FAUSTUS. Why, how now, sir knight? What, hanged by the   135
  horns? This is most horrible. Fie, fie, pull in your head,
  for shame. Let not all the world wonder at you.

BENVOLIO. Zounds, doctor, is this your villainy?

FAUSTUS. O, say not so, sir. The doctor has no skill,

No art, no cunning to present these lords   140
Or bring before this royal Emperor
The mighty monarch, warlike Alexander.
If Faustus do it, you are straight resolved
In bold Actaeon's shape to turn a stag. –
And therefore, my lord, so please your Majesty,   145
I'll raise a kennel of hounds shall hunt him so
As all his footmanship shall scarce prevail
To keep his carcass from their bloody fangs.
Ho, Belimoth, Argiron, Ashtaroth!

BENVOLIO. Hold, hold! Zounds, he'll raise up a kennel of   150
    devils, I think, anon. – Good my lord, entreat for me. –
    [BENVOLIO *is attacked by* DEVILS.] 'Sblood, I am never
    able to endure these torments.

EMPEROR. Then, good Master Doctor,
    Let me entreat you to remove his horns.   155
    He has done penance now sufficiently.

FAUSTUS. My gracious lord, not so much for injury done
    to me as to delight your Majesty with some mirth hath
    Faustus justly requited this injurious knight; which
    being all I desire, I am content to remove his horns. – 160
    Mephistopheles, transform him. [MEPHISTOPHELES
    removes the horns.] And hereafter, sir, look you speak well
    of scholars.

BENVOLIO [*aside*]. Speak well of ye? 'Sblood, an scholars
    be such cuckold-makers to clap horns of honest men's   165
    heads o' this order, I'll ne'er trust smooth faces and small
    ruffs more. But, an I be not revenged for this, would I might
    be turned to a gaping oyster and drink nothing but salt
    water.

    [*Exit from the window.*]

EMPEROR. Come, Faustus. While the Emperor lives,   170
    In recompense of this thy high desert
    Thou shalt command the state of Germany
    And live beloved of mighty Carolus.

    Exeunt omnes.

[IV.ii]

Enter BENVOLIO, MARTINO, FREDERICK, *and* SOLDIERS.

MARTINO. Nay, sweet Benvolio, let us sway thy thoughts
    From this attempt against the conjurer.

BENVOLIO. Away! You love me not, to urge me thus.
    Shall I let slip so great an injury
    When every servile groom jests at my wrongs   5
    And in their rustic gambols proudly say,
    'Benvolio's head was graced with horns today'?
    O, may these eyelids never close again
    Till with my sword I have that conjurer slain!
    If you will aid me in this enterprise,   10
    Then draw your weapons and be resolute.
    If not, depart. Here will Benvolio die
    But Faustus' death shall quit my infamy.

FREDERICK. Nay, we will stay with thee, betide what may,
    And kill that doctor if he come this way.   15

BENVOLIO. Then, gentle Frederick, hie thee to the grove,
    And place our servants and our followers
    Close in an ambush there behind the trees.
    By this, I know, the conjurer is near;
    I saw him kneel and kiss the Emperor's hand   20
    And take his leave, laden with rich rewards.
    Then, soldiers, boldly fight. If Faustus die,
    Take you the wealth; leave us the victory.

FREDERICK. Come, soldiers, follow me unto the grove.
    Who kills him shall have gold and endless love.   25

    Exit FREDERICK *with the* SOLDIERS.

BENVOLIO. My head is lighter than it was by th' horns,
    But yet my heart's more ponderous than my head
    And pants until I see that conjurer dead.

MARTINO. Where shall we place ourselves, Benvolio?

BENVOLIO. Here will we stay to bide the first assault.   30
    O, were that damnèd hellhound but in place,
    Thou soon shouldst see me quit my foul disgrace.

Enter FREDERICK.

FREDERICK. Close, close! The conjurer is at hand
    And all alone comes walking in his gown.
    Be ready, then, and strike the peasant down.   35

BENVOLIO. Mine be that honour, then. Now, sword, strike home!
    For horns he gave, I'll have his head anon.

Enter FAUSTUS, *with the false head.*

MARTINO. See, see, he comes.

BENVOLIO. No words. This blow ends all.
    Hell take his soul! His body thus must fall.

    [*He strikes* FAUSTUS.]

FAUSTUS [*falling*]. O!   40

FREDERICK. Groan you, Master Doctor?

BENVOLIO. Break may his heart with groans! Dear Frederick, see,
    Thus will I end his griefs immediately.

MARTINO. Strike with a willing hand.

    [BENVOLIO *strikes off* FAUSTUS's *false head.*]

                His head is off!

BENVOLIO. The devil's dead. The Furies now may laugh.   45

FREDERICK. Was this that stern aspect, that awful frown,
    Made the grim monarch of infernal spirits
    Tremble and quake at his commanding charms?

MARTINO. Was this that damnèd head whose heart conspired
    Benvolio's shame before the Emperor?   50

BENVOLIO. Ay, that's the head, and here the body lies,
    Justly rewarded for his villainies.

FREDERICK. Come, let's devise how we may add more shame
    To the black scandal of his hated name.

BENVOLIO. First, on his head, in quittance of my wrongs,   55
    I'll nail huge forkèd horns and let them hang

Within the window where he yoked me first,
That all the world may see my just revenge.

MARTINO. What use shall we put his beard to?

BENVOLIO. We'll sell it to a chimney-sweeper. It will wear   60
out ten birchen brooms, I warrant you.

FREDERICK. What shall his eyes do?

BENVOLIO. We'll put out his eyes, and they shall serve for
buttons to his lips to keep his tongue from catching cold.

MARTINO. An excellent policy. And now, sirs, having   65
divided him, what shall the body do?

[FAUSTUS *rises.*]

BENVOLIO. Zounds, the devil's alive again!

FREDERICK. Give him his head, for God's sake!

FAUSTUS. Nay, keep it. Faustus will have heads and hands,
Ay, all your hearts, to recompense this deed.   70
Knew you not, traitors, I was limited
For four-and-twenty years to breathe on earth?
And had you cut my body with your swords,
Or hewed this flesh and bones as small as sand,
Yet in a minute had my spirit returned,   75
And I had breathed a man made free from harm.
But wherefore do I dally my revenge?
Ashtaroth, Belimoth, Mephistopheles!

Enter MEPHISTOPHELES *and other devils* [BELIMOTH
and ASHTAROTH].

Go horse these traitors on your fiery backs,
And mount aloft with them as high as heaven;   80
Thence pitch them headlong to the lowest hell.
Yet stay. The world shall see their misery,
And hell shall after plague their treachery.
Go, Belimoth, and take this caitiff hence,
And hurl him in some lake of mud and dirt.   85
[*To* ASHTAROTH.] Take thou this other; drag him
through the woods

Amongst the pricking thorns and sharpest briers,
Whilst with my gentle Mephistopheles
This traitor flies unto some steepy rock
That, rolling down, may break the villain's bones   90
As he intended to dismember me.
Fly hence. Dispatch my charge immediately.

FREDERICK. Pity us, gentle Faustus. Save our lives!

FAUSTUS. Away!

FREDERICK.   He must needs go that the devil drives.

Exeunt SPIRITS *with the* KNIGHTS [*on their backs*].
Enter the ambushed SOLDIERS.

FIRST SOLDIER. Come, sirs. Prepare yourselves in readiness;   95
Make haste to help these noble gentlemen.
I heard them parley with the conjurer.

SECOND SOLDIER. See where he comes. Dispatch, and kill
the slave.

FAUSTUS. What's here? An ambush to betray my life?
Then, Faustus, try thy skill. Base peasants, stand!   100

[*Trees come between* FAUSTUS *and the* SOLDIERS.]

For lo, these trees remove at my command
And stand as bulwarks 'twixt yourselves and me
To shield me from your hated treachery.
Yet to encounter this your weak attempt,
Behold an army comes incontinent.   105

FAUSTUS *strikes the door, and enter a* DEVIL *playing on a
drum, after him another bearing an ensign, and divers with weapons;*
MEPHISTOPHELES *with fireworks. They set upon the*
SOLDIERS *and drive them out.* [*Exit* FAUSTUS.]

[IV.iii]

Enter at several doors BENVOLIO, FREDERICK, *and* MARTINO,
*their heads and faces bloody and besmeared with mud and dirt, all having
horns on their heads.*

MARTINO. What ho, Benvolio!

BENVOLIO.   Here. What, Frederick, ho!

FREDERICK. O, help me, gentle friend. Where is Martino?

MARTINO. Dear Frederick, here,
    Half smothered in a lake of mud and dirt
    Through which the Furies dragged me by the heels.   5

FREDERICK. Martino, see! Benvolio's horns again.

MARTINO. O misery! How now, Benvolio?

BENVOLIO. Defend me, heaven. Shall I be haunted still?

MARTINO. Nay, fear not, man. We have no power to kill.

BENVOLIO. My friends transformèd thus! O hellish spite!   10
    Your heads are all set with horns.

FREDERICK.   You hit it right.
    It is your own you mean. Feel on your head.

BENVOLIO [*feeling his head*]. Zounds, horns again!

MARTINO. Nay, chafe not, man, we all are sped.

BENVOLIO. What devil attends this damned magician,   15
    That, spite of spite, our wrongs are doublèd?

FREDERICK. What may we do, that we may hide our shames?

BENVOLIO. If we should follow him to work revenge,
    He'd join long asses' ears to these huge horns
    And make us laughing-stocks to all the world.   20

MARTINO. What shall we then do, dear Benvolio?

BENVOLIO. I have a castle joining near these woods,
    And thither we'll repair and live obscure
    Till time shall alter this our brutish shapes.
    Sith black disgrace hath thus eclipsed our fame,   25
    We'll rather die with grief than live with shame.

Exeunt omnes.

[IV.iv]

Enter FAUSTUS, *and the* HORSE-COURSER, *and*
MEPHISTOPHELES.

HORSE-COURSER [*offering money*]. I beseech your worship,
accept of these forty dollars.

FAUSTUS. Friend, thou canst not buy so good a horse for so
small a price. I have no great need to sell him, but if thou
likest him for ten dollars more, take him, because I see thou   5
hast a good mind to him.

HORSE-COURSER. I beseech you, sir, accept of this. I am a
very poor man and have lost very much of late by horseflesh,
and this bargain will set me up again.

FAUSTUS. Well, I will not stand with thee. Give me the   10
money. [*He takes the money.*] Now, sirrah, I must tell you
that you may ride him o'er hedge and ditch, and spare him
not. But do you hear? In any case ride him not into the
water.

HORSE-COURSER. How, sir, not into the water? Why, will   15
he not drink of all waters?

FAUSTUS. Yes, he will drink of all waters. But ride him not
into the water. O'er hedge and ditch, or where thou wilt,
but not into the water. Go bid the ostler deliver him unto
you, and remember what I say.   20

HORSE-COURSER. I warrant you, sir. – O, joyful day! Now
am I a made man for ever.

Exit.

FAUSTUS. What art thou, Faustus, but a man condemned to die?
Thy fatal time draws to a final end.
Despair doth drive distrust into my thoughts.   25
Confound these passions with a quiet sleep.
Tush! Christ did call the thief upon the cross;
Then rest thee, Faustus, quiet in conceit.

He sits to sleep. Enter the HORSE-COURSER, *wet.*

HORSE-COURSER. O, what a cozening doctor was this!
    I, riding my horse into the water, thinking some hidden   30
    mystery had been in the horse, I had nothing under me
    but a little straw and had much ado to escape drowning.
    Well, I'll go rouse him and make him give me my forty
    dollars again. – Ho, sirrah doctor, you cozening scab!
    Master Doctor, awake, and rise, and give me my money   35
    again, for your horse is turned to a bottle of hay. Master
    Doctor! (*He pulls off his leg.*) Alas, I am undone! What shall
    I do? I have pulled off his leg.

FAUSTUS. O, help, help! The villain hath murdered me.

HORSE-COURSER. Murder or not murder, now he has but   40
    one leg I'll outrun him and cast this leg into some ditch
    or other.

    [*Exit with the leg.*]

FAUSTUS. Stop him, stop him, stop him! – Ha, ha, ha!
    Faustus hath his leg again, and the Horse-courser a bundle
    of hay for his forty dollars.   45

    Enter WAGNER.

    How now, Wagner, what news with thee?

WAGNER. If it please you, the Duke of Vanholt doth earnestly
    entreat your company and hath sent some of his men to
    attend you with provision fit for your journey.

FAUSTUS. The Duke of Vanholt's an honourable gentleman,   50
    and one to whom I must be no niggard of my cunning.
    Come away.

    Exeunt.

[IV.v]
Enter CLOWN [ROBIN], DICK, HORSE-COURSER, *and*
a CARTER.

CARTER. Come, my masters, I'll bring you to the best beer
    in Europe. – What ho, Hostess! – Where be these whores?

Enter HOSTESS.

HOSTESS. How now, what lack you? What, my old guests, welcome!

ROBIN [*aside to* DICK]. Sirrah Dick, dost thou know why   5
I stand so mute?

DICK [*aside to* ROBIN]. No, Robin, why is 't?

ROBIN [*aside to* DICK]. I am eighteen pence on the score. But say nothing. See if she have forgotten me.

HOSTESS [*seeing* ROBIN.] Who's this that stands so solemnly   10
by himself? [*To* ROBIN.] What, my old guest?

ROBIN. O, Hostess, how do you? I hope my score stands still.

HOSTESS. Ay, there's no doubt of that, for methinks you make no haste to wipe it out.

DICK. Why, Hostess, I say, fetch us some beer.   15

HOSTESS. You shall, presently. – Look up into th' hall there, ho!

Exit.

DICK. Come, sirs, what shall we do now till mine Hostess comes?

CARTER. Marry, sir, I'll tell you the bravest tale how a   20
conjurer served me. You know Doctor Fauster?

HORSE-COURSER. Ay, a plague take him! Here's some on 's have cause to know him. Did he conjure thee, too?

CARTER. I'll tell you how he served me. As I was going to Wittenberg t' other day with a load of hay, he met me and   25
asked me what he should give me for as much hay as he could eat. Now, sir, I thinking that a little would serve his turn, bade him take as much as he would for three farthings. So he presently gave me my money and fell to eating; and, as I am a cursen man, he never left eating till   30
he had eat up all my load of hay.

ALL. O monstrous! Eat a whole load of hay!

ROBIN. Yes, yes, that may be, for I have heard of one that has
    eat a load of logs.

HORSE-COURSER. Now, sirs, you shall hear how villain-   35
    ously he served me. I went to him yesterday to buy a horse
    of him, and he would by no means sell him under forty dollars.
    So, sir, because I knew him to be such a horse as would run
    over hedge and ditch and never tire, I gave him his money.
    So when I had my horse, Doctor Fauster bade me ride him   40
    night and day and spare him no time. 'But', quoth he, 'in
    any case ride him not into the water.' Now, sir, I, thinking
    the horse had had some quality that he would not have me
    know of, what did I but rid him into a great river? And when
    I came just in the midst, my horse vanished away, and I sat   45
    straddling upon a bottle of hay.

ALL. O brave doctor!

HORSE-COURSER. But you shall hear how bravely I served
    him for it. I went me home to his house, and there I found
    him asleep. I kept a halloing and whooping in his ears, but   50
    all could not wake him. I, seeing that, took him by the leg
    and never rested pulling till I had pulled me his leg quite off,
    and now 'tis at home in mine hostry.

ROBIN. And has the doctor but one leg, then? That's excellent, for
    one of his devils turned me into the likeness of an ape's face.   55

CARTER. Some more drink, Hostess!

ROBIN. Hark you, we'll into another room and drink a while,
    and then we'll go seek out the doctor.

    Exeunt omnes.

[IV.vi]

Enter the DUKE OF VANHOLT, *his [pregnant]* DUCHESS,
FAUSTUS, *and* MEPHISTOPHELES [*and* SERVANTS].

DUKE. Thanks, Master Doctor, for these pleasant sights. Nor
    know I how sufficiently to recompense your great deserts

in erecting that enchanted castle in the air, the sight whereof
so delighted me as nothing in the world could please me
more.   5

FAUSTUS. I do think myself, my good lord, highly recom-
pensed in that it pleaseth your Grace to think but well of
that which Faustus hath performed. – But, gracious lady,
it may be that you have taken no pleasure in those sights.
Therefore, I pray you tell me what is the thing you most   10
desire to have; be it in the world, it shall be yours. I have
heard that great-bellied women do long for things are rare
and dainty.

DUCHESS. True, Master Doctor, and, since I find you so kind,
I will make known unto you what my heart desires to have.   15
And were it now summer, as it is January, a dead time of
the winter, I would request no better meat than a dish of
ripe grapes.

FAUSTUS. This is but a small matter.
[*Aside to* MEPHISTOPHELES.] Go, Mephistopheles, away!   20

Exit MEPHISTOPHELES.

Madam, I will do more than this for your content.

Enter MEPHISTOPHELES *again with the grapes.*

Here. Now taste ye these. They should be good, for they
come from a far country, I can tell you.

[*The* DUCHESS *tastes the grapes.*]

DUKE. This makes me wonder more than all the rest, that
at this time of the year, when every tree is barren of his   25
fruit, from whence you had these ripe grapes.

FAUSTUS. Please it your Grace, the year is divided into two
circles over the whole world, so that, when it is winter with
us, in the contrary circle it is likewise summer with them,
as in India, Saba, and such countries that lie far east,   30
where they have fruit twice a year. From whence, by means
of a swift spirit that I have, I had these grapes brought, as
you see.

DUCHESS. And, trust me, they are the sweetest grapes that
    e'er I tasted.   35

    The CLOWN[S] *bounce at the gate, within.*

DUKE. What rude disturbers have we at the gate?
    Go pacify their fury. Set it ope,
    And then demand of them what they would have.

    They knock again and call out to talk with FAUSTUS.
    [*A* SERVANT *goes to the gate.*]

SERVANT. Why, how now, masters, what a coil is there!
    What is the reason you disturb the duke?   40

DICK [*offstage*]. We have no reason for it. Therefore, a fig
    for him!

SERVANT. Why, saucy varlets, dare you be so bold?

HORSE-COURSER [*offstage*]. I hope, sir, we have wit enough
    to be more bold than welcome.   45

SERVANT. It appears so. Pray be bold elsewhere, and trouble
    not the duke.

DUKE [*to the* SERVANT]. What would they have?

SERVANT. They all cry out to speak with Doctor Faustus.

CARTER [*offstage*]. Ay, and we will speak with him.   50

DUKE. Will you, sir? – Commit the rascals.

DICK [*offstage*]. Commit with us? He were as good commit
    with his father as commit with us.

FAUSTUS. I do beseech your Grace, let them come in.
    They are good subject for a merriment.   55

DUKE. Do as thou wilt, Faustus. I give thee leave.

FAUSTUS. I thank your Grace.

    [*The Servant opens the gate.*] *Enter the* CLOWN [ROBIN], DICK,
    CARTER, *and* HORSE-COURSER.

                       Why, how now, my good friends?

'Faith, you are too outrageous. But come near;
I have procured your pardons. Welcome all!

ROBIN. Nay, sir, we will be welcome for our money, and we   60
will pay for what we take. – What ho! Give's half a dozen
of beer here, and be hanged.

FAUSTUS. Nay, hark you, can you tell me where you are?

CARTER. Ay, marry, can I. We are under heaven.

SERVANT. Ay, but, sir saucebox, know you in what place?   65

HORSE-COURSER. Ay, ay, the house is good enough to drink
in. Zounds, fill us some beer, or we'll break all the barrels in
the house and dash out all your brains with your bottles.

FAUSTUS. Be not so furious. Come, you shall have beer. –
My lord, beseech you give me leave a while.   70
I'll gage my credit 'twill content your Grace.

DUKE. With all my heart, kind doctor. Please thyself.
Our servants and our court's at thy command.

FAUSTUS. I humbly thank your Grace. – Then fetch some beer.

HORSE-COURSER. Ay, marry, there spake a doctor indeed,   75
and, 'faith, I'll drink a health to thy wooden leg for that word.

FAUSTUS. My wooden leg? What dost thou mean by that?

CARTER. Ha, ha, ha! Dost hear him, Dick? He has forgot his leg.

HORSE-COURSER. Ay, ay. He does not stand much upon
that.   80

FAUSTUS. No, 'faith, not much upon a wooden leg.

CARTER. Good Lord, that flesh and blood should be so frail
with your worship! Do not you remember a horse-courser
you sold a horse to?

FAUSTUS. Yes, I remember I sold one a horse.   85

CARTER. And do you remember you bid he should not ride
into the water?

FAUSTUS. Yes, I do very well remember that.

CARTER. And do you remember nothing of your leg?

FAUSTUS. No, in good sooth.   90

CARTER. Then, I pray, remember your curtsy.

FAUSTUS [*making a curtsy*]. I thank you, sir.

CARTER. 'Tis not so much worth. I pray you tell me one thing.

FAUSTUS. What's that?

CARTER. Be both your legs bedfellows every night together?   95

FAUSTUS. Wouldst thou make a Colossus of me, that thou
     askest me such questions?

CARTER. No, truly, sir, I would make nothing of you. But
     I would fain know that.

     Enter HOSTESS *with drink*.

FAUSTUS. Then, I assure thee, certainly they are.   100

CARTER. I thank you. I am fully satisfied.

FAUSTUS. But wherefore dost thou ask?

CARTER. For nothing, sir. But methinks you should have a
     wooden bedfellow of one of 'em.

HORSE-COURSER. Why, do you hear, sir? Did not I pull   105
     off one of your legs when you were asleep?

FAUSTUS. But I have it again now I am awake. Look you
     here, sir.

     [*He shows them his legs.*]

ALL. O, horrible! Had the doctor three legs?

CARTER. Do you remember, sir, how you cozened me and   110
     eat up my load of –

     FAUSTUS *charms him dumb*.

DICK. Do you remember how you made me wear an ape's –

     [FAUSTUS *charms him dumb*.]

HORSE-COURSER. You whoreson conjuring scab, do you
    remember how you cozened me with a ho –

    [FAUSTUS *charms him dumb.*]

ROBIN. Ha' you forgotten me? You think to carry it away   115
    with your 'hey-pass' and 'repass'. Do you remember
    the dog's fa –

    [FAUSTUS *charms him dumb.*] *Exeunt* CLOWNS.

HOSTESS. Who pays for the ale? Hear you, Master Doctor,
    now you have sent away my guests, I pray, who shall pay
    me for my a –   120

    [FAUSTUS *charms her dumb.*]

    Exit HOSTESS.

DUCHESS [*to the* DUKE]. My lord,
    We are much beholding to this learnèd man.

DUKE. So are we, madam, which we will recompense
    With all the love and kindness that we may.
    His artful sport drives all sad thoughts away.   125

    Exeunt.

Act V

[v.i]

Thunder and lightning. Enter DEVILS *with covered dishes.* MEPHISTO-PHELES *leads them into* FAUSTUS's *study. Then enter* WAGNER.

WAGNER. I think my master means to die shortly.
    He has made his will and given me his wealth:
    His house, his goods, and store of golden plate,
    Besides two thousand ducats ready coined.
    I wonder what he means. If death were nigh,   5
    He would not frolic thus. He's now at supper
    With the scholars, where there's such belly-cheer
    As Wagner in his life ne'er saw the like.
    And see where they come. Belike the feast is done.

Exit. Enter FAUSTUS, MEPHISTOPHELES, *and two or three* SCHOLARS.

FIRST SCHOLAR. Master Doctor Faustus, since our con-   10
    ference about fair ladies – which was the beautifullest in all
    the world – we have determined with ourselves that Helen
    of Greece was the admirablest lady that ever lived. There-
    fore, Master Doctor, if you will do us so much favour as
    to let us see that peerless dame of Greece, whom all the   15
    world admires for majesty, we should think ourselves
    much beholding unto you.

FAUSTUS. Gentlemen,
    For that I know your friendship is unfeigned,
    It is not Faustus' custom to deny   20
    The just request of those that wish him well:
    You shall behold that peerless dame of Greece,
    No otherwise for pomp or majesty
    Than when Sir Paris crossed the seas with her
    And brought the spoils to rich Dardania.   25

Be silent then, for danger is in words.

[MEPHISTOPHELES *goes to the door.*] *Music sound.* MEPHIS-
TOPHELES *brings in* HELEN. *She passeth over the stage.*

SECOND SCHOLAR. Was this fair Helen, whose admirèd worth
    Made Greece with ten years' wars afflict poor Troy?

THIRD SCHOLAR. Too simple is my wit to tell her worth,
    Whom all the world admires for majesty.   30

FIRST SCHOLAR. Now we have seen the pride of nature's work,
    We'll take our leaves, and for this blessèd sight
    Happy and blest be Faustus evermore.

FAUSTUS. Gentlemen, farewell. The same wish I to you.

    Exeunt SCHOLARS. *Enter an* OLD MAN.

OLD MAN. O gentle Faustus, leave this damnèd art,   35
    This magic, that will charm thy soul to hell
    And quite bereave thee of salvation!
    Though thou hast now offended like a man,
    Do not persever in it like a devil.
    Yet, yet thou hast an amiable soul,   40
    If sin by custom grow not into nature.
    Then, Faustus, will repentance come too late;
    Then thou art banished from the sight of heaven.
    No mortal can express the pains of hell.
    It may be this my exhortation   45
    Seems harsh and all unpleasant. Let it not,
    For, gentle son, I speak it not in wrath
    Or envy of thee, but in tender love
    And pity of thy future misery;
    And so have hope that this my kind rebuke,   50
    Checking thy body, may amend thy soul.

FAUSTUS. Where art thou, Faustus? Wretch, what hast thou done?
    Hell claims his right, and with a roaring voice
    Says, 'Faustus, come! Thine hour is almost come.'

    MEPHISTOPHELES *gives him a dagger.*

    And Faustus now will come to do thee right.   55

[FAUSTUS *prepares to stab himself.*]

OLD MAN. O, stay, good Faustus, stay thy desperate steps!
    I see an angel hover o'er thy head,
    And with a vial full of precious grace
    Offers to pour the same into thy soul.
    Then call for mercy and avoid despair.   60

FAUSTUS. O friend, I feel thy words to comfort my distressèd soul.
    Leave me a while to ponder on my sins.

OLD MAN. Faustus, I leave thee, but with grief of heart,
    Fearing the enemy of thy hapless soul.

    Exit.

FAUSTUS. Accursèd Faustus, wretch, what hast thou done?   65
    I do repent, and yet I do despair.
    Hell strives with grace for conquest in my breast.
    What shall I do to shun the snares of death?

MEPHISTOPHELES. Thou traitor, Faustus, I arrest thy soul
    For disobedience to my sovereign lord.   70
    Revolt, or I'll in piecemeal tear thy flesh.

FAUSTUS. I do repent I e'er offended him.
    Sweet Mephistopheles, entreat thy lord
    To pardon my unjust presumption,
    And with my blood again I will confirm   75
    The former vow I made to Lucifer.

MEPHISTOPHELES. Do it then, Faustus, with unfeignèd heart,
    Lest greater dangers do attend thy drift.

    [FAUSTUS *cuts his arm and writes with his blood.*]

FAUSTUS. Torment, sweet friend, that base and agèd man
    That durst dissuade me from thy Lucifer,   80
    With greatest torment that our hell affords.

MEPHISTOPHELES. His faith is great. I cannot touch his soul.
    But what I may afflict his body with
    I will attempt, which is but little worth.

FAUSTUS. One thing, good servant, let me crave of thee   85
    To glut the longing of my heart's desire:

That I may have unto my paramour
That heavenly Helen, which I saw of late,
Whose sweet embraces may extinguish clear
Those thoughts that do dissuade me from my vow,   90
And keep my vow I made to Lucifer.

MEPHISTOPHELES. This, or what else my Faustus shall desire,
    Shall be performed in twinkling of an eye.

Enter HELEN *again* [*brought in by* MEPHISTOPHELES], *passing
over between two* CUPIDS.

FAUSTUS. Was this the face that launched a thousand ships
    And burnt the topless towers of Ilium?   95
    Sweet Helen, make me immortal with a kiss.

[*They kiss.*]

Her lips suck forth my soul. See where it flies!
Come, Helen, come, give me my soul again.

[*They kiss again.*]

Here will I dwell, for heaven is in these lips,
And all is dross that is not Helena.   100
I will be Paris, and for love of thee
Instead of Troy shall Wittenberg be sacked,
And I will combat with weak Menelaus,
And wear thy colours on my plumèd crest.
Yea, I will wound Achilles in the heel   105
And then return to Helen for a kiss.
O, thou art fairer than the evening's air,
Clad in the beauty of a thousand stars.
Brighter art thou than flaming Jupiter
When he appeared to hapless Semele,   110
More lovely than the monarch of the sky
In wanton Arethusa's azure arms;
And none but thou shalt be my paramour.

Exeunt.

[V.ii]

Thunder. Enter LUCIFER, BEELZEBUB, *and* MEPHISTOPHELES
[*above*].

LUCIFER. Thus from infernal Dis do we ascend
    To view the subjects of our monarchy,
    Those souls which sin seals the black sons of hell,
    'Mong which as chief, Faustus, we come to thee,
    Bringing with us lasting damnation   5
    To wait upon thy soul. The time is come
    Which makes it forfeit.

MEPHISTOPHELES.   And this gloomy night
    Here in this room will wretched Faustus be.

BEELZEBUB. And here we'll stay
    To mark him how he doth demean himself.   10

MEPHISTOPHELES. How should he, but in desperate lunacy?
    Fond worldling, now his heart-blood dries with grief;
    His conscience kills it, and his labouring brain
    Begets a world of idle fantasies
    To overreach the devil. But all in vain.   15
    His store of pleasures must be sauced with pain.
    He and his servant Wagner are at hand,
    Both come from drawing Faustus' latest will.
    See where they come.

    Enter FAUSTUS *and* WAGNER.

FAUSTUS. Say, Wagner. Thou hast perused my will;   20
    How dost thou like it?

WAGNER. Sir, so wondrous well
    As in all humble duty I do yield
    My life and lasting service for your love.

    Enter the SCHOLARS.

FAUSTUS. Gramercies, Wagner. – Welcome, gentlemen.

    [*Exit* WAGNER.]

FIRST SCHOLAR. Now, worthy Faustus, methinks your
    looks are changed.   25

FAUSTUS. O gentlemen!

SECOND SCHOLAR. What ails Faustus?

FAUSTUS. Ah, my sweet chamber-fellow! Had I lived with
thee, then had I lived still, but now must die eternally. Look,   30
sirs, comes he not? Comes he not?

FIRST SCHOLAR. O my dear Faustus, what imports this fear?

SECOND SCHOLAR. Is all our pleasure turned to melancholy?

THIRD SCHOLAR [*to the other* SCHOLARS]. He is not well
with being over-solitary.   35

SECOND SCHOLAR. If it be so, we'll have physicians, and
Faustus shall be cured.

THIRD SCHOLAR [*to* FAUSTUS]. 'Tis but a surfeit, sir. Fear
nothing.

FAUSTUS. A surfeit of deadly sin, that hath damned both   40
body and soul.

SECOND SCHOLAR. Yet, Faustus, look up to heaven, and
remember mercy is infinite.

FAUSTUS. But Faustus' offence can ne'er be pardoned. The
serpent that tempted Eve may be saved, but not Faustus.   45
O gentlemen, hear with patience, and tremble not at my
speeches. Though my heart pant and quiver to remember
that I have been a student here these thirty years, O, would
I had never seen Wittenberg, never read book! And what
wonders I have done, all Germany can witness, yea, all   50
the world, for which Faustus hath lost both Germany and
the world, yea, heaven itself – heaven, the seat of God, the
throne of the blessed, the kingdom of joy – and must remain
in hell for ever. Hell, O, hell for ever! Sweet friends, what
shall become of Faustus, being in hell for ever?   55

SECOND SCHOLAR. Yet, Faustus, call on God.

FAUSTUS. On God, whom Faustus hath abjured? On God,
whom Faustus hath blasphemed? O my God, I would
weep, but the devil draws in my tears. Gush forth blood   60
instead of tears, yea, life and soul. O, he stays my tongue!

I would lift up my hands, but see, they hold 'em, they
hold 'em.

ALL. Who, Faustus?

FAUSTUS. Why, Lucifer and Mephistopheles. O gentlemen,   65
I gave them my soul for my cunning.

ALL. O, God forbid!

FAUSTUS. God forbade it indeed, but Faustus hath done it.
For the vain pleasure of four-and-twenty years hath Faustus
lost eternal joy and felicity. I writ them a bill with mine   70
own blood. The date is expired. This is the time, and he
will fetch me.

FIRST SCHOLAR. Why did not Faustus tell us of this before, that
divines might have prayed for thee?

FAUSTUS. Oft have I thought to have done so, but the devil   75
threatened to tear me in pieces if I named God, to fetch
me body and soul if I once gave ear to divinity. And now
'tis too late. Gentlemen, away, lest you perish with me.

SECOND SCHOLAR. O, what may we do to save Faustus?

FAUSTUS. Talk not of me, but save yourselves and depart.   80

THIRD SCHOLAR. God will strengthen me. I will stay with
Faustus.

FIRST SCHOLAR [*to the* THIRD SCHOLAR]. Tempt not God,
sweet friend, but let us into the next room and pray for him.

FAUSTUS. Ay, pray for me, pray for me! And what noise so   85
ever you hear, come not unto me, for nothing can rescue me.

SECOND SCHOLAR. Pray thou, and we will pray that God
may have mercy upon thee.

FAUSTUS. Gentlemen, farewell. If I live till morning, I'll visit
you; if not, Faustus is gone to hell.   90

ALL. Faustus, farewell.

    Exeunt SCHOLARS.

MEPHISTOPHELES. Ay, Faustus, now thou hast no hope
    of heaven;
    Therefore despair. Think only upon hell,
    For that must be thy mansion, there to dwell.

FAUSTUS. O thou bewitching fiend, 'twas thy temptation   95
    Hath robbed me of eternal happiness.

MEPHISTOPHELES. I do confess it, Faustus, and rejoice.
    'Twas I that, when thou wert i'the way to heaven,
    Dammed up thy passage. When thou took'st the book
    To view the Scriptures, then I turned the leaves   100
    And led thine eye.
    What, weep'st thou? 'Tis too late. Despair, farewell!
    Fools that will laugh on earth must weep in hell.

Exit. Enter the GOOD ANGEL *and the* BAD ANGEL *at
several doors.*

GOOD ANGEL. O Faustus, if thou hadst given ear to me,
    Innumerable joys had followed thee.   105
    But thou didst love the world.

BAD ANGEL.   Gave ear to me,
    And now must taste hell's pains perpetually.

GOOD ANGEL. O, what will all thy riches, pleasures, pomps
    Avail thee now?

BAD ANGEL.   Nothing but vex thee more,
    To want in hell, that had on earth such store.   110

Music while the throne descends.

GOOD ANGEL. O, thou hast lost celestial happiness,
    Pleasures unspeakable, bliss without end.
    Hadst thou affected sweet divinity,
    Hell or the devil had had no power on thee.
    Hadst thou kept on that way, Faustus, behold   115
    In what resplendent glory thou hadst set
    In yonder throne, like those bright shining saints,
    And triumphed over hell. That hast thou lost.
    And now, poor soul, must thy good angel leave thee.
    The jaws of hell are open to receive thee.   120

[The throne ascends.] Exit [GOOD ANGEL]. *Hell is discovered.*

BAD ANGEL. Now, Faustus, let thine eyes with horror stare
    Into that vast perpetual torture-house.
    There are the Furies tossing damned souls
    On burning forks; their bodies boil in lead.
    There are live quarters broiling on the coals,   125
    That ne'er can die. This ever-burning chair
    Is for o'er-tortured souls to rest them in.
    These that are fed with sops of flaming fire
    Were gluttons, and loved only delicates.
    And laughed to see the poor starve at their gates.   130
    But yet all these are nothing. Thou shalt see
    Ten thousand tortures that more horrid be.

FAUSTUS. O, I have seen enough to torture me!

BAD ANGEL. Nay, thou must feel them, taste the smart of all.
    He that loves pleasure must for pleasure fall.   135
    And so I leave thee, Faustus, till anon;
    Then wilt thou tumble in confusion.

    Exit.

    The clock strikes eleven.

FAUSTUS. O Faustus,
    Now hast thou but one bare hour to live,
    And then thou must be damned perpetually.   140
    Stand still, you ever-moving spheres of heaven,
    That time may cease and midnight never come!
    Fair nature's eye, rise, rise again, and make
    Perpetual day; or let this hour be but
    A year, a month, a week, a natural day,   145
    That Faustus may repent and save his soul!
    O lente, lente currite noctis equi!
    The stars move still; time runs; the clock will strike;
    The devil will come, and Faustus must be damned.
    O, I'll leap up to heaven! Who pulls me down?   150
    One drop of blood will save me. O, my Christ!
    Rend not my heart for naming of my Christ!
    Yet will I call on him. O, spare me, Lucifer!

Where is it now? 'Tis gone;
And see, a threat'ning arm, an angry brow.   155
Mountains and hills, come, come and fall on me,
And hide me from the heavy wrath of heaven!
No? Then will I headlong run into the earth.
Gape, earth! O, no, it will not harbour me.
You stars that reigned at my nativity,   160
Whose influence hath allotted death and hell,
Now draw up Faustus like a foggy mist
Into the entrails of yon labouring cloud,
That when you vomit forth into the air,
My limbs may issue from your smoky mouths,   165
But let my soul mount and ascend to heaven.

The watch strikes.

O, half the hour is past! 'Twill all be past anon.
O, if my soul must suffer for my sin,
Impose some end to my incessant pain.
Let Faustus live in hell a thousand years,   170
A hundred thousand, and at last be saved.
No end is limited to damnèd souls.
Why wert thou not a creature wanting soul?
Or why is this immortal that thou hast?
O, Pythagoras' *metempsychosis*, were that true,   175
This soul should fly from me and I be changed
Into some brutish beast.
All beasts are happy, for, when they die,
Their souls are soon dissolved in elements;
But mine must live still to be plagued in hell.   180
Curst be the parents that engendered me!
No, Faustus, curse thyself. Curse Lucifer,
That hath deprived thee of the joys of heaven.

The clock strikes twelve.

It strikes, it strikes! Now, body, turn to air,
Or Lucifer will bear thee quick to hell.   185
O soul, be changed into small waterdrops,
And fall into the ocean, ne'er be found!

Thunder, and enter the DEVILS.

O, mercy, heaven, look not so fierce on me!
Adders and serpents, let me breathe a while!
Ugly hell, gape not. Come not, Lucifer!   190
I'll burn my books. O, Mephistopheles!

Exeunt.

[V.iii]

Enter the SCHOLARS.

FIRST SCHOLAR. Come, gentlemen, let us go visit Faustus,
    For such a dreadful night was never seen
    Since first the world's creation did begin.
    Such fearful shrieks and cries were never heard.
    Pray heaven the doctor have escaped the danger.   5

SECOND SCHOLAR. O, help us, heaven! See, here are
    Faustus' limbs,
    All torn asunder by the hand of death.

THIRD SCHOLAR. The devils whom Faustus served have
    torn him thus.
    For, 'twixt the hours of twelve and one, methought
    I heard him shriek and call aloud for help,   10
    At which self time the house seemed all on fire
    With dreadful horror of these damnèd fiends.

SECOND SCHOLAR. Well, gentlemen, though Faustus' end
    be such
    As every Christian heart laments to think on,
    Yet, for he was a scholar, once admired   15
    For wondrous knowledge in our German schools,
    We'll give his mangled limbs due burial;
    And all the students, clothed in mourning black,
    Shall wait upon his heavy funeral.

Exeunt.

[Epilogue]

Enter CHORUS.

CHORUS. Cut is the branch that might have grown full straight,
    And burnèd is Apollo's laurel bough
    That sometime grew within this learnèd man.
    Faustus is gone. Regard his hellish fall,
    Whose fiendful fortune may exhort the wise   5
    Only to wonder at unlawful things,
    Whose deepness doth entice such forward wits
    To practise more than heavenly power permits.

    [*Exit.*]

Terminat hora diem; terminat author opus.

Glossary

Acheron – river of woe in the underworld

affected – pretended

Agrippa – famous Renaissance conjuror

Albanus – Pietro d'Albano, Italian philosopher and magician of the thirteenth century

Alexander's love . . . Oenone's death – Paris (otherwise Alexandros) deserted the nymph Oenone, who later refused to save his life, and killed herself in remorse

Almaine rutters – German cavalry

amiable – worthy of love

anagrammatised – made into anagrams

Analytics – Aristotle's works on proof in rhetoric

antics – clowns

Antwerp's bridge, fiery keel at – fireship used to destroy a bridge during the Siege of Antwerp (1585)

Apollo – classical god of poetry, and also of prophecy

Arethusa – nymph transformed by the lustful god Alpheus into a spring (the point of Faustus' reference is unclear)

Aware – here, beware

awful – full of awe: awe-inspiring

Bacon – Roger Bacon, famous thirteenth-century philosopher and magician

basilisk – fabled reptile, with a fatal stare

beads – prayer beads

beaten silk – embroidered silk

bell, book, and candle – the instruments of excommunication

Bene . . . logices – 'to dispute well is the aim of logic'

bevers – snacks or drinks between meals

bills – medical prescriptions

bottle of hay – bundle of hay

bounce – knock

canvass every quiddity – go into every detail

Carolus – Charles V, Holy Roman Emperor (1519-56)

chafer – portable carrier for fire

chafing – double-meaning of scolding and rubbing against

characters – here, magical symbols

Che serà, serà – 'what will be, will be' (proverbial)

coelum igneum et crystallinum – the fiery and crystalline spheres of the medieval universe

commit – take into custody

compass – devise

concave – here, cavity in a rock

conceit, quiet in – of calm mind

conjunctions, oppositions – planets at their nearest and opposite points respectively

consistory – forum for ecclesiastical discussion

Consummatum est – 'it is finished': the dying words of Christ on the cross

corpus naturale . . . mobile – 'a natural and changeable body'

counters – tokens (i.e., of no monetary value)

cozening – cheating

cull – select (for quality, or slaughter)

cursen – christened

Dardania – Troy

Diana . . . Acteon – reference to the myth of the boastful huntsman turned to a stag for intruding on Diana bathing naked

Dis – kingdom of the underworld

Ecce signum – 'behold the sign'

Emden, seignory of – governor of this German trading port

empyreal heaven – that is, the part of the heavens which may be observed

empyreal orb – outermost sphere of the Ptolemaic universe

except – unless

Exhaereditare . . . nisi – 'a father cannot disinherit his son unless' (see Introduction, p. xxi)

fain – willingly, gladly

flagitious – wicked

fond – foolish, idle

fustian – bombast, rant

gage – pledge

Galen – leading Greek authority on medicine

glass windows – here, spectacles
gratulate – show pleasure at
gravelled – confounded, refuted
great-bellied – pregnant
gridirons – instruments of torture, aptly confused by Robin
    with 'guilders' (which see)
groom – here, any underling
guilders – Dutch coins
gyves – shackles
halters – here, nooses, as for hanging a man
Hecate – underworld goddess of crossroads (the usual site of gallows)
hey-pass – juggling term, here casual abuse
hippocras – wine flavoured with spices
hogshead – cask containing 64 gallons
hold belly hold – to the belly's full capacity
Homo, fuge – 'fly, man'
horse-bread – fodder made with coarse grains
horse-courser – horse dealer
hostry – hostelry, tavern
Ilium – Troy
incontinent – instantly
intelligentia – controlling intelligence
int'rest – 'interest' in the legal and financial sense
iterating – repetition
Jerome – compiler of sixth-century version of the Bible
Kill-devil – colloquial term for a reckless youth, possibly also for rum
Lade – load, set about
licentiate – person licensed to study for a higher degree
Lollards – 'heretical' would-be reformers of the medieval church
Maledicat Dominus – 'may the Lord curse him'
March-beer – strong beer, brewed for lengthy maturation
Maro's – Virgil's, the Roman poet
Martlemas-beef – salted beef (killed at Martinmas, in November)
massy entrails – solid inner core
meet with – be even with, get my revenge upon
Menelaus – husband to Helen of Troy
metempsychosis – doctrine of the transmigration of souls after death,
    said to have been originated by the Greek philosopher
    Pythagoras

Musaeus – Aeneas's guide to the underworld in the *Aeneid*

O lente . . . equi – 'run slowly, you horses of the night'

Oeconomy – Aristotle's reputed studies of household management

old philosophers – consigned to inhabit Limbo rather than Heaven or Hell

On kai me on – 'being and not being'

order, o' this – in this way

Ovid's flea – that is, one who can creep into women's private places

Parma, Prince of – Catholic governor of the Spanish Netherlands

peerless – without equal

Penelope – faithful wife to Odysseus in the *Odyssey*

pension – bare subsistence

per accidens – fortuitously (that is, as only an indirect effect of Faustus's conjuration)

Per inaequalem . . . totius – 'through unequal motion in relation to the whole'

Peter's feast – saint's day of St. Peter, 29 June

Phlegethon – burning river in the underworld

Physic – medicine

pickedevants – short goatee beards

pitchy – black and odorous

placket – opening in female dress: hence, colloquially, vagina

plaud, appeal our – seek applause

pottage – porridge

precisian – a puritan ('precise' in religious observance)

presence – that is, presence chamber, room for receiving supplicants

privy chamber – ruler's private suite

proper shapes – distinctive shapes

prove – put to the test

quartered – that is, quartered bodies

quasi vestigiis insistere – 'as if walking in our tracks'

Qui mihi discipulus – 'you who are my pupil' (opening line of schoolbook)

quiet poles – unmoving poles (of the Ptolemaic universe)

Quin redis . . . imagine – 'Why have you not returned, Mephistopheles, in the form of a friar?'

Rector – that is, of the university

rest beholding – remaining indebted

rouse, took his – got very drunk

Saba – that is, Sheba, the Queen who tested Solomon's wisdom

sadness, in good – truly, earnestly

Sanctobulorum . . . tostu Mephistopheles – largely meaningless: Robin is trying to emulate Faustus' incantations

'Sblood – abbreviated form of oath, 'by Christ's blood'

Semele – lover of Jupiter, struck dead by lightning when he answered her plea to reveal himself in all his glory

shadows – ghostly forms

Si peccasse . . . veritas – 'if we say that we have no sin, we deceive ourselves, and the truth is not in us' (but John's epistle then stresses God's readiness to forgive)

Si una . . . valorum rei – 'if one thing is willed to two persons, one of them shall have the thing itself, the other the value of the thing' (see Introduction, p. xxi)

sic probo – 'I prove it thus' (concluding phrase in disputation)

Sint mihi . . . dicatus Mephistopheles – 'May the gods of Acheron smile on me! May the triple-spirited Jehovah be gone! Welcome, spirits of air, fire and water! Be propitious, Beelzebub, Prince of the East and of fiery Hell, and Demogorgon, so that Mephistopheles may appear and rise! Why do you delay? By Jehovah, by Gehenna, by the holy water which I now sprinkle, by the sign of the cross which I now make, and by our prayers, may Mephistopheles now arise at our bidding'

situ et tempore – in direction and time

Snails – abbreviated oath, 'by his nails' (Christ's on the cross)

Solamen . . . doloris – 'it is a comfort to the miserable to have companions in their misery'

speculation – study

spheres – here, the concentric circles containing the elements in the Ptolomaic universe

spite of spite – in spite of anything we can do

state – throne (an actual property in the Elizabethan theatre)

statutes decretal – papal decrees

stavesacre – flower seeds used to treat lice infestation

stays – stops

Stipendium . . . mors est – 'the wages of sin is death' (St. Paul adds, 'but the free gift of God is eternal life)

stoups – filled tankards

Styx – river across which dead souls were rowed to the underworld *subtle air* – thin air

summum bonum – greatest good

Summum . . . sanitas – 'health is the greatest good of medicine'

Terminat . . . opus – 'the hour ends the day, the author ends his work'

termine – furthest point, boundary

tester – sixpenny piece

Trasimene – site of battle where the Romans were defeated by Hannibal

Trier – town on the Mosel river in western Germany

triumphs – celebratory civic pageants

ubi desinit . . . medicus – 'where the philosopher leaves off, there the doctor begins'

Vanholt – German duchy adjoining Wittenberg

vengeance, with a – 'my curse going with you'

water, bring his – bring his urine (to test)

wear out – outlast

welkin – sky

whippincrust – spiced wine, same as *hippocras* (which see)

zodiac, poles of the – in the Ptolomaic universe, the axle on which the planets appear to move through the constellations of the zodiac